Jewelry Making
with RESIN

Jewelry Making
with RESIN

Theresa D. Abelew

Waukesha, WI

Dedication

*To Evangeline & Emerson,
for reminding me of the joy and
excitement in creative exploration.
I love you.*

Kalmbach Books
21027 Crossroads Circle
Waukesha, Wisconsin 53186
www.JewelryAndBeadingStore.com

Numbered and lettered step-by-step photos by the author.
All other photography © 2017 Kalmbach Books except
where otherwise noted.

The jewelry designs in *The Absolute Beginners Guide:
Jewelry Making with Resin* are the copyrighted property
of the author, and they may not be taught or sold without
permission. Please use them for your education and
personal enjoyment only.

Please follow appropriate health and safety measures
when working with materials and equipment. Some
general guidelines are presented in this book, but
always read and follow manufacturers' instructions.

Every effort has been made to ensure the accuracy of
the information presented; however, the publisher is not
responsible for any injuries, losses, or other damages that
may result from the use of the information in this book.

Published in 2017
21 20 19 18 17   1 2 3 4 5

Manufactured in China

ISBN: 978-1-62700-402-2
EISBN: 978-1-62700-403-9

Editor: Erica Barse
Book Design: Lisa Bergman
Photographer: William Zuback
Proofreader: Dana Meredith

Library of Congress Control Number: 2016943712

Contents

PROJECTS

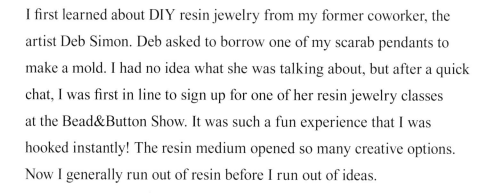

Welcome to the wonderful, albeit potentially messy, world of resin

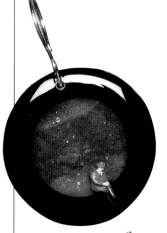

I first learned about DIY resin jewelry from my former coworker, the artist Deb Simon. Deb asked to borrow one of my scarab pendants to make a mold. I had no idea what she was talking about, but after a quick chat, I was first in line to sign up for one of her resin jewelry classes at the Bead&Button Show. It was such a fun experience that I was hooked instantly! The resin medium opened so many creative options. Now I generally run out of resin before I run out of ideas.

This book is a starter guide to exploring resin techniques. Sure, you can complete each of the projects as directed, but try breaking down the individual projects—mix and match the different techniques to discover and showcase your individual sense of style. Don't be afraid to search for inspiration outside of your comfort zone. I've used a number of doodads and thingamabobs that I picked up by chance. If it doesn't work, maybe it can be cut apart or reused for a different resin project.

Due to curing times, working with resin is a slow process—don't rush it. If your piece isn't working the way you hoped, walk away and let it cure for a couple days. When you come back, you'll have a fresh perspective—and potentially new ideas.

Enjoy!
—Theresa

Basics

MATERIALS

Resin
There are many resins available for the home jewelry maker. The majority of resins come in two parts: the resin and the hardener. The mixing ratios, drying and curing times, clean up, etc. can all vary, depending on the manufacturer. While all the projects in the book are completed with ICE Resin (www.rangerink.com/shopiceresin), most two-part epoxy resins will behave in the same, or very similar manner. Just be sure to read the manufacturer's instructions first.

Findings
The main focus of this book is the resin. The chains, crystals, findings, jump rings, and chain mail were mostly things I already had on hand. Sometimes having a stash comes in rather handy. Use whatever clasps, earring wires, chains, or findings that suit your style, taste, and budget.

Wood
The majority of wood used can be found at your local hardware or home improvement store. The only "exotic" wood I used was the African Padauk for the "Jellyfish Pendant," p. 86, which was found at a local woodworking shop. But you can substitute the exotic wood for more common hardwoods, like oak, maple, or walnut, which can be found at local hardware or home improvement stores.

Paper
Most papers used in this book are common solid-colored scrapbook papers. Handmade and specialty papers can make a beautiful addition to your resin jewelry; just be sure to do a test spot before committing. Some paper will become translucent when coated with resin and others might change colors or lose interesting texture and details. You can also try sealing the paper before applying the resin. While there are specialty sealers designed for just this thing, you can also try a coat of Mod Podge or Elmers School Glue. Experiment with one or two thin coats (apply the second coat in an overlapping direction, up-and-down, then side-to-side, and don't forget to seal the edges). Make sure the sealer is completely dry before applying any resin.

Measuring Cups and Stir Sticks
Plastic medicine cups are great for ensuring that you have accurate measurements while pouring the resin and hardener. Stir sticks can be as simple as wooden popsicle/craft sticks, or plastic paddle stir sticks especially designed for stirring resin. Cups and sticks can be found at www.rangerink.com/shopiceresin, or online retailers.

Supplies
Wire, sponge brushes, wood, tools, wooden dowels, screw eyes, sandpaper, paint stir sticks, lath, and safety gear: Local hardware or home improvement store

Fiber washers: Home Depot

Eyelets, ribbon, fabric, and resin dyes: local bead, hobby, or craft store

Packaging tape, plastic bags, wax paper: local big box stores

Quilling paper and quilling tool: Quilling Superstore, www.quillingsuperstore.com or local craft store

Triple Glow Powder: Glo-nation, www.glonation.com

Jewelry findings, chains, bezels, crystals, beads, and jump rings: local bead or craft stores

---

Basics

SETUP

No matter how careful you are, resin is a messy medium. Whether you have a studio or are working at the kitchen table, a little prep work to protect your workspace will go a long way.

Work Surface

Make sure your work surface is smooth and level. Resin is a self-leveling liquid, so if your surface is tilted or heavily textured, the resin will mimic the surface and either run down the side of your project or potentially pick up the texture. I use a large vintage drafting table as workspace, and while it is level, the wood isn't perfectly smooth. To compensate, I lay a piece of tempered glass (24x15 in./ 61x38cm) on a towel. The towel protects the table from getting scratched from the glass's sharp edges.

I picked up several sheets of glass from a garage sale of a person who custom built fish tanks (hence, the raw edges). Alternative places to find tempered glass are old stereo cabinets (remember those?). Back in the 80s and 90s, everyone had one of those glass and pressboard cabinets with the glass door and glass top covering the turntable. I have a few of those as well, and those edges are polished and smooth. Most glass supply companies or local hardware stores will also have some sort of tempered glass available (and I'd recommend asking for finished edges).

PROTECTIVE COVERINGS

So, now you have a level and smooth surface. How do you keep it resin-free? If you work with resin directly on that surface, resin will eventually adhere to it. And while you can clean it off with razor blades, a simpler solution is an ordinary plastic garbage bag. The regular kitchen trash bags that come in a roll will last you for ages. If you are careful, most of the cured resin will peel right off. Eventually the bags will be too speckled with cured resin to use as a work surface, but they can still be used for their original purpose. (Just turn them inside out, so if any resin peels off the bag, it will already be inside the bag.) For my space, I lay the bag over my glass panel and tuck the bag under the top and bottom edge of the glass. Pull the plastic tight to remove any wrinkles or creases.

TIP While working directly on top of the garbage bag, be sure not to lay wet resin over anything printed on the plastic. The drying resin will transfer any print onto itself, leaving your cured resin piece with random bits of print.

I also like being able to move my pieces around, so sometimes I will work on a large Ziploc-type of bag. The cured resin peels off cleanly. The resin that was touching the plastic surface will have a shiny finish, but it will also pick up any wrinkles or print from the bag.

Waxed Paper

Waxed paper should be reserved for "light-duty" resin projects, because it is possible to soak and oversaturate waxed paper, which in turn will adhere to your project. However, when used correctly, resin cured in contact with waxed paper will peel away with a matte effect. This is because some of the wax from the paper will adhere to the surface of the resin. It can be an interesting effect; however, if you wish to add additional layers of resin, it will act as a wax resist, and the resin will not evenly coat the surface. Give the piece a light sanding to remove any wax residue if you wish to apply additional layers of resin.

Pot Lids

Yes, you read that right! Once your resin is ready to dry and cure, you want to make sure it won't be disturbed by pets, kids, dust, or anything else that might mar the smooth surface. Old glass pot lids are perfect for this. I used to use a box until one day my cat got into the studio and claimed that box for himself. I placed the box over a table full of wet resin and when I removed it the next day, I discovered the entire batch was compromised with cat hair. Once cured, whatever dust or pet hair is dropped in the wet resin will STAY in the cured resin. While most clear resin can be cut into to remove debris and then refilled seamlessly, it's easier to avoid any unwanted "embellishments" in the first place.

TOOLS AND SAFETY GEAR

Particulate Respirator

This is a must-have safety item! Any time you are cutting, sanding, or cleaning up dust and debris from cured resin, wear a respirator. While wet sanding will help keep dust down (and out of your lungs), it's better to be safe than sorry. Always wipe down your work surface with a damp paper towel to remove as much resin dust as possible.

Safety Glasses

If you are cutting or using power tools, wear safety glasses. While it is unlikely that any of these resin projects will shatter, I did snap my fair share of drill bits while writing this book.

Other Items

If you have long hair, tie it back! Remember all those horror stories your shop teacher told you about long hair and the drill press? It's totally true for power drills, too. Be sure to tie back long hair, remove jewelry, and secure any loose-fitting clothing. If you need a reminder, wrap a hair tie (or several) around your drill, so you will see it when you pick it up. Be sure to remove any rings as well; while it's not as much of a concern for the drill, if you get any resin on faceted gemstones (like a wedding ring), you won't be happy with the results! See the "Bezel Embellishment Pendant," p. 21, to see what a drop of resin did to a faceted crystal.

Gloves (Plastic, Vinyl, or Latex)

Most resin instructions will highly recommend wearing gloves while working with resin. Some people will have reactions to wet resin if it comes in contact with their skin; however, wet resin on your gloves can easily be overlooked and if you subconsciously play with your hair, well ... you get the idea. None of the step-by-step images show me wearing gloves, but you can certainly do so—just be mindful.

RESIN TECHNIQUES

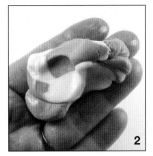

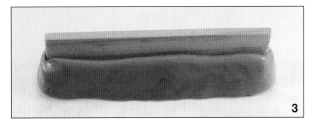

Using Two-Part Silicone Molding Compound

Silicone molding compound is easy to use and sets up fast. Before you begin, make sure the item you will be molding is ready to use. Use your hands to roll equal-sized balls of part A and part B of the compound. (Check the manufacturer's instructions to verify the correct ratio for your brand of compound [1].) Knead the two balls together [2], blending the colors into a uniform consistency. Roll the compound into an oval or circular shape slightly larger than the item being molded. Flatten the back of the mold against your work surface. Press the item (in this case, a cut-off section from a paint stir stick) into the compound, taking care not to press all the way through the compound. Use your fingers to press the edges of the compound evenly into all sides of the object [3]. Do not remove the object until the compound has set per the manufacturer's instructions.

Open-Sided Molds

With some projects, like the "Lath Pendant," p. 75, you will need to have a more "adjustable" type of mold. Follow the instructions as previously indicated to mix the compound. Form a rectangular shape slightly wider than the lath board while flattening the back against the work surface [4]. Keep the board parallel to the work surface, press the board into the molding compound [5], and use your fingers to press up the three edges of the compound around the lath. Maintain the parallel position of the lath by skimming it in place with a notebook, craft sticks, or other item.

TIP

If you push the object too hard and punch through the bottom of the mold, you can try to salvage the mold by burnishing a piece of packaging tape to the bottom. Keep in mind silicone is supposed to be non-stick, so this isn't a fool-proof or longterm plan. Resin will still leak out, but it will be at a much slower rate, and you might be able to get a few decent copies from the mold. But you might be better off recasting the mold.

Removing Resin from a Mold

While silicone molds are sturdy enough to be used over and over, they are still somewhat of a delicate tool. A fingernail can easily cut into or tear a mold apart. While resin will release from a silicone mold fairly easily, sometimes it needs a bit of help.

Gently use your fingernail to pry and loosen all the edges of the resin from the mold [1]. If the resin begins to stretch and distort, it's not dry enough. Replace it as best as you can and allow it to dry a bit longer before removing. Once dry, slowly pull the resin away from the impression, lay it on a flat surface [2], and allow it to cure.

If the mold is deep (like the mold created for the "Stir Stick Necklace," p. 42), gently loosen the edges of the resin and use your thumbs to carefully push the back of the mold and release the resin impression.

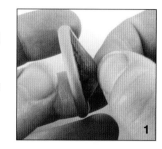
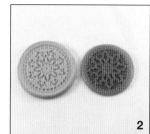

Mixing Resin

Verify the manufacturer's recommended mixing ratio of your resin to hardener. For my brand, it's 1:1, so I use a permanent marker to mark the measurement points on the medicine cup before pouring [3]. Get eye level with the cup and pour in the resin. (If you over- or under-pour, you may need to re-mark your second measurement to maintain proper ratio.) Pour in the hardener and use a stir stick to gently mix the two parts together. Be sure to scrape along the bottom and edges of the cup to make sure it is well mixed [4]. Use smooth and steady movements; if you whip them together like scrambled eggs, you'll end up with a resin pot full of bubbles.

Let the mixed resin rest for a minute or two to allow any bubbles to rise to the surface. Most bubbles will pop on their own, but if they need a little encouragement, you can breathe warm air over them, or use a warm–hot hair dryer at a low speed.

Coloring Resin

I have tinted resin with a number of different items to varying degrees of success. Fine powders work wonderfully, from powdered dyes, to spices, or even old makeup; use a toothpick to add small amounts of powder to the wet resin and stir thoroughly. Because it takes so little powder to color the resin, I've never had an issue with the resin not curing properly, although I've been told it is possible. I've had mixed results with liquid colorants, like oil paints. The resin still cures properly, but mixing it thoroughly enough to eliminate "oil paint bubbles" is a bit tricky. But don't be afraid to experiment, and just remember—a little colorant goes a long way!

TIP During the cold Wisconsin winters, my resin will become thick, sluggish, and prone to air bubbles when mixed. A quick warm water bath eliminates those problems. Place enough water in a microwave-safe bowl to cover about half of the height of the resin and hardener bottles. Zap the water a few minutes, until warm. Then, place the bottles in warm water and let them soak while you prepare your workspace and materials. After a few minutes, remove the bottles and tip to check the consistency. You should notice the liquid has thinned and moves much quicker, which means it will stir much easier, and you'll end up with markedly fewer bubbles.

Applying Resin

When using a sponge or disposable brush, treat the resin just like paint. Dip the brush into the resin, wipe the excess on the edge of the cup, and apply a thin, even coat. Because of the viscosity of resin, "paint" in only one direction, since painting back and forth will produce air bubbles.

When using a craft stick (or toothpick), you can carefully pour the resin on the component and then use the stick to coat the component—or you can hold the container above the component while using the stick to scoop and drizzle small amounts of resin on the component (my preferred method). Then coat by pushing the resin in front of the stick until the *resin* reaches the edge of the component, not the stick (or the resin may overflow).

Clean Up

Check the manufacturer's instructions for recommended clean up. Depending on the brand, a bit of rubbing alcohol on a paper towel can do wonders. For other brands, rubbing alcohol is a catalyst to "speed cure" resin, shortening its pot life and solidifying it within a few minutes (also superheating it to the point of smoking, making for an extremely dangerous situation).

To remove wet resin from hands and most surfaces, baby wipes are the quickest and easiest choice. Depending on the brand, wipes may leave a bit of an oily residue on work surfaces or projects, but a little soap and water will clean that right up.

Dry Time vs. Cure Time

Dry and cure times vary depending on brand of resin, and conditions within the studio. During humid summer weather, resin will take longer to cure than during dry, cold winters. However, I will vary the cure time to fit the need of the technique. For example, the resin I used in this book (Ice Resin) is fully cured after three days. But the resin will usually dry in 8–12 hours, leaving the resin flexible, but slightly soft without being sticky. I can press my fingernail into the resin, but the resin will slowly spring back to a smooth surface—kind of like a memory foam pillow. This comes in handy if I'm working on a final piece that I want to be a bit curvy, like a bracelet. I will let the piece *dry* flat, but will move the piece to *cure* closer to the preferred finished shape. For example, when making a bracelet, I will move a dry piece to a bracelet mandrel so the bracelet will cure into more of an oval shape.

Using a Miter Box

A miter box is a simple woodworking tool that is used with a saw to create precise 90-degree or 45-degree cuts. Depending on the orientation of your resin component (against the fence or flat), you can create angled cuts or beveled edges—for example, see the image of the saw. The blue layer is the front of the component. A component laid against the fence will result in a 45-degree beveled edge. A component laid flat will result in a 90-degree flat edge.

To use: Secure the miter box. Some have a lip that will hold it in place along the bench edge. Others can be mounted onto a workbench. Mark the item to be cut with a permanent marker. Place the item against the side of the box closest to you (the front fence). Align the cut mark with the appropriate saw guide slot, and secure the item in place with your non-dominant hand or a clamp. Saw.

If you are new to using a miter box, don't expect the cut to be perfect. You can fix wonky sawing with a bit of sanding. While you are just starting out, it might be helpful to cut the items a little on the large side, and sand them down to the desired final size.

TIP If you use a clamp, make sure you have room to move the saw without hitting the clamp.

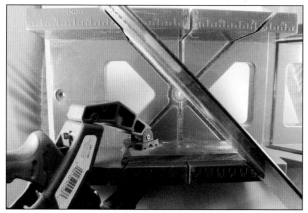
Component laid against the fence

Component laid flat

Place the saw into the coordinating guide slots. Depending on your method of securing the item and its size, you can either lay it flat or stand it up against the front fence. Try both ways to see which is easier for you. Use a gentle, steady pressure to saw the item while keeping the saw in the guide slots.

Sanding

Sanding is the process of smoothing a surface by gradually using finer grits of sandpaper. In this book, "working through the grits" refers to sanding with the roughest grit (the low number, like 80) and moving up the finer grits (to a high number, like 2000).

To wet-sand, place the sandpaper on a flat surface, add a few drops of water, and then sand as usual. The water both extends the life of the paper and helps trap dust.

SANDPAPER GRITS USED IN THIS BOOK	
80	dry
220	
320	wet/dry
400	
800	
1000	
1500	
2000	

When sanding wood, sand with the grain for best results. For resin, however, I recommend the figure-8 pattern. Secure the sandpaper with your hand, or a bit of tape on a flat surface. Hold the component on the sandpaper and move it in a figure-8 pattern. This pattern helps maintain even pressure on all sides of the component and will prevent it from being sanded unevenly. Once the component is smooth and has a consistent sanding pattern over the entire surface, move to the next finer grit and repeat. Continue to the recommended or desired finish.

Drilling

For all the projects in this book, I used drill bits ranging from 1/16–1/2 in. (1.5mm–1.3cm).

Use a permanent marker to mark the placement for the holes. Use your fingers to twist a small drill bit into the mark to create a divot for the drill. Place the component on a piece of scrap wood and secure it with your non-dominant hand. Place the smallest drill bit into the divot, hold the drill perpendicular to the component, and gently press the drill trigger. Drill all the holes with the first size bit, and then re-drill with a larger size bit (it doesn't have to be the next step up; resin is easily drilled and you can skip a size or two between bits). Continue working your way up to the final size bit.

TIP For some projects (like the "Base Block Bracelet," p. 82), drilling through wood with large bits can be a challenge. If you try to secure the squares of wood in place with your hands, there is a good chance you won't be able to hold it in place, and it will tear up your hands. Try using a clamp with a bit of spare wood to secure the component in place, sparing your fingers.

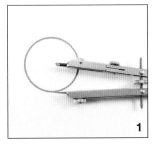

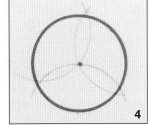

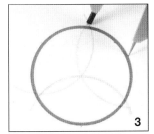

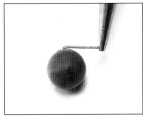

Finding the Center of a Circle

Lay your compass over the circle, adjust and lock the compass width to roughly half the diameter of your circle [1]. Place the needle leg on the edge of the circle and mark the arc through the center of the circle. Move the needle leg about one-third of the way around the circle, and draw a second arc [2]. Repeat to draw a third arc [3]. The point where all three lines intersect is the center of the circle [4].

If your estimate is a little off when setting your compass, and you end up with a triangle instead of a clear intersection of arcs, your center point is the middle of the triangle [5] (or you can adjust the compass and redraw the arcs).

JEWELRY BASICS

Plain Loops

1 Trim the wire or headpin ⅜ in. (1cm) above the bead. Make a right-angle bend close to the bead.

2 Grab the wire's tip with roundnose pliers. The tip of the wire should be flush with the pliers. Roll the wire to form a half-circle. Release the wire.

3 Reposition the pliers in the loop and continue rolling.

4 The finished loop should form a centered circle above the bead.

Wrapped Loops

1 Make sure you have at least 1¼ in. (3.2cm) of wire above the bead. With the tip of your chainnose pliers, grasp the wire directly above the bead. Bend the wire (above the pliers) into a right angle.

2 Using roundnose pliers, position the jaws in the bend.

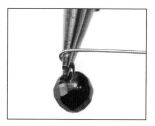

3 Bring the wire over the top jaw of the roundnose pliers.

4 Reposition the pliers' lower jaw snugly into the loop. Curve the wire downward around the bottom of the roundnose pliers. This is the first half of a wrapped loop.

5 Position the chainnose pliers' jaws across the loop.

6 Wrap the wire around the wire stem, covering the stem between the loop and the top bead. Trim the excess wire and press the cut end close to the wraps with chainnose pliers.

Opening and Closing Loops or Jump Rings

1 Hold the loop or jump ring with two pairs of chainnose pliers or chainnose and roundnose pliers, as shown.

2 To open the loop or jump ring, bring one pair of pliers toward you and push the other pair away. String materials on the open loop or jump ring. Reverse the steps to close the open loop or jump ring.

Crimping

1 Position the crimp bead in the hole of the crimping pliers that is closest to the handle.

2 Holding the wires apart, squeeze the tool to compress the crimp bead, making sure one wire is on each side of the dent.

3 Place the crimp bead in the front hole of the tool, and position it so the dent is facing outward. Squeeze the tool to fold the crimp in half.

4 Tug on the wires to ensure that the crimp is secure.

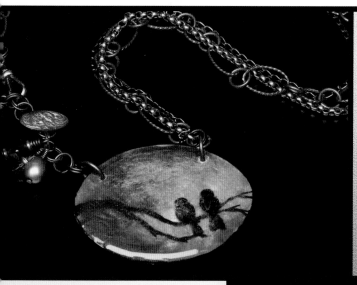

Projects

PROJECT 1

Photo Bezel necklace

One of the first applications I learned when starting with resin was how to mount a photo in a bezel. While resized photos are an obvious choice, don't overlook bits of old letters, maps, drawings, or other small objects to create a collage that showcases your individual taste and style.

WHAT YOU'LL NEED

Resin Component Supplies

- Bezel (size and shape determined by design)
- Resin
- Pencil
- Photo print
- Scissors or craft knife
- Paintbrush and craft stick
- Elmer's school glue or clear sealant
- Scrap cardstock or printer paper

Jewelry Supplies

- Beads or stones in assorted shapes
- Beading wire
- Headpin
- Large jump ring
- **2 crimp beads**
- Two-part clasp
- Roundnose pliers, chainnose pliers, wire cutters, crimping pliers

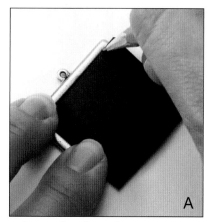

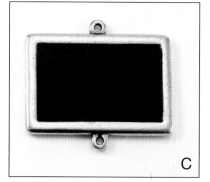

1 Create a bezel template: For square or rectangular bezels, use a scissors or craft knife to cut a right angle out of the cardstock or paper. Align the 90-degree angle with a corner of the bezel. Use a pencil to mark the top [**A**] and bottom inside edge [**B**] along one side of the bezel. Trim that edge and check the fit, adjust if necessary. Mark the fourth edge of the bezel, and trim to fit [**C**].

2 While it may be easier to get a more accurate template with cardstock, I find lightweight paper is helpful for "framing" an image. Place the photo over a light table or window you can align your template to your frame your image. Either hold in place and trim, or use a pen to trace the template before trimming the photo.

3 Test the fit of the photo, and adjust as needed. Remember, it's easier to trim a little at a time rather than start over because you cut off too much of the image.

4 Use a small paintbrush and a little bit of glue or sealant to seal the edges of the image. If you don't seal the edges, resin may get between the layers of the photo and discolor or leave marks along some of the edges. Let the image dry.

5 Apply a light layer of resin along the bottom of the bezel, and leave a small amount of resin across the bezel. Insert the sealed image into the resin at an angle. Push the image through the resin and along the base of the bezel, while pushing the image against the backplate. This will help reduce air bubbles trapped between the bezel's backplate and the image.

TIP To further eliminate air bubbles, use a craft stick to burnish the image to the bezel. Start in the middle of the image, and push the craft stick along the image to the edge of the bezel. Pop or remove any bubbles that emerge.

6 Add in resin to completely cover the image. The dome height of the resin depends on the brand and viscosity of the resin. Clean up any drips or overflow while wet. Move the bezel away from any spills. Cover and allow the resin to cure per manufacturer's instructions.

7 Complete the necklace (see "Jewelry Basics," p. 14): Cut two lengths of beading wire the length of your desired necklace plus a few inches. String a crimp bead and half of the clasp over the end of both wires, and go back through the crimp bead. Crimp the clasp half to the necklace. String two strands of beads in the pattern of your choice, and crimp the other clasp half to the other two wires in the same way. String a few beads on the headpin and make a plain loop. Attach the bead dangle to the bottom loop of the resin component, and attach the top loop of the component to both strands of the necklace with a jump ring.

PROJECT 2

Bezel Embellishment Pendant

One of the great things about resin is that you never have to be done playing with it. I was testing out new resins a few years back and used one of my favorite photos of my grandparents (yes, those really are my grandparents, Gilbert and Rita). As much as I love this photo, I wanted to give it a little pop. So, here are two easy embellishments to spice up a cured piece of resin: rub-on transfers and flat-back crystals. I discovered rub-on transfers at a local scrapbook store. The scrapbooking section of your local hobby and craft store is an indispensible treasure trove of ideas for resin projects.

WHAT YOU'LL NEED

Resin Component Supplies
- Resin component with a cured, smooth surface
- Rub-on transfer
- Scissors
- Craft stick
- Flat-back crystals
- Resin
- Sponge brush
- Toothpicks

Jewelry Supplies
- Crystals in assorted shapes
- Fancy chain
- Snap-on bail
- **5–10** headpins
- **3** jump rings
- Two-part clasp
- Roundnose pliers, chainnose pliers, wire cutters

Transfer Substitute

If you can't find rub-on transfers, temporary tattoos will work, too. (Yes, the same kind you might have used as a kid!) Apply the tattoo to clear resin, just like you would to skin, using a damp wash cloth.

1 Make sure the surface of the resin is clean and dirt free.

2 Find the rub-on transfer you wish to apply. Keep in mind, transfer sheets are easy to cut to size or can be altered so you can use just what you want. As you can see in my example, "Lovely" doesn't quite fit inside the bezel, but "Love" does. Use a scissors to trim the transfer to fit.

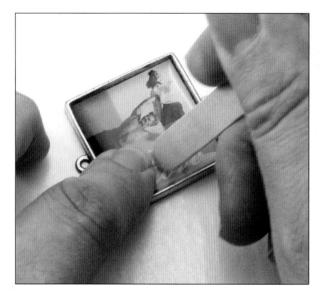

3 Once in place, firmly press the transfer down with your finger. Use a craft stick or burnisher to rub the letters onto the cured resin. Make sure the sheet doesn't shift, or you may misalign your transfer.

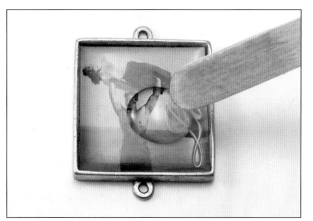

4 After the transfer has been burnished to the surface of the resin, carefully remove the transfer sheet.

5 Apply a light coat of resin to seal the transfer in place. Allow the resin to cure.

TIP Crystals can be a bit tricky to work with; you need enough resin to hold them in place, but not too much to cover them. If you do get any resin on a crystal, the facets appear to melt away, leaving a colored circle in its place.

6 Play with the arrangement, colors, and sizes of flat-back crystals on your cured pendant. This process will be easier the flatter (less-domed) the cured piece is.

7 Remove the crystals and make sure the surface of the resin is clean and dirt-free. Use a sponge brush to lightly coat the surface with wet resin.

TIP To help reduce bubbles, keep brush strokes to a minimum, and brush on the resin from only one direction (I'm going left to right).

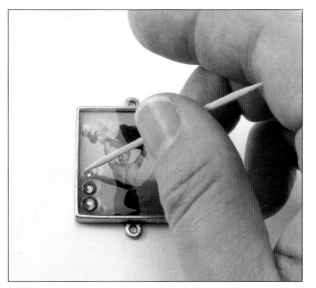

8 Place the crystals as close to their final location as possible. I've found the easiest way for me to pick up the crystals is to have them crystal side up on the table. Then slightly dampen your finger, and press your finger onto the crystal. It will stick to your finger and you can place the crystals, one by one, onto the wet resin surface. Use a clean toothpick to make any minute final adjustments.

9 Clean up any wet resin overflow. Cover and allow the resin to cure.

10 Complete the necklace (see "Jewelry Basics," p. 14): Attach a snap-on bail to the top ring of the bezel. Cut two pieces of chain the length of your desired necklace, and thread both through the snap-on bail. Use jump rings to attach a clasp half to both ends of the chains. Use a jump ring to secure several various lengths of chain to the bottom ring of the bezel to create a chain tassel. String a crystal bead on a headpin, and make a plain loop. Attach the plain loop to a section of the chain tassel. Repeat with various colors of crytals to coordinate with the flat-back crystals and image.

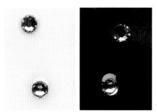

The crystals on the top half of the samples are properly set in resin. The bottom crystals have resin covering their facets, leaving the crystals looking like shiny spots.

PROJECT 3
Texture Sheet Ring

Silicone texture sheets are often used to create textures on metal and polymer clays, and those same silicone texture sheets can also be used with resin. Even silicone baking or ice cube trays will work (my "Walking Dead" ice cube tray has never held water, but many friends have received resin zombie body parts). Whenever I work on a resin project, I like to keep my silicone texture sheets nearby so I can use them with any leftover resin.

Resin Component Supplies
- Silicone texture sheet
- Powder dye
- Q-tip, small paintbrush, or toothbrush
- Resin
- Toothpick or craft stick
- Bezel ring
- Circle template
- Permanent marker
- Scissors or craft knife
- Uncooked rice and container

1 Tint the texture sheet: To help amplify the pattern of a texture sheet, I like to apply powdered dye directly to the sheet. Use a Q-tip with a bit of old eye shadow or dye powder and lightly rub over the surface of the texture sheet. Tap or blow off any excess powder.

 TIP It's not necessary to use any dye on the texture sheet, but I have found it helps the resin release a little easier from some of the deeper or more detailed textures.

2 Mix your resin and add powder in the desired color (see "Coloring Resin," p. 11). Spread the resin over the prepared surface of the texture sheet: Use a toothpick or craft stick to evenly distribute the resin and pop any bubbles. Because I generally use these textured-resin sheets inside bezels, the resin can be spread fairly thin.

3 Let the resin dry, and then peel it off of the texture sheet (see "Dry Time vs. Cure Time," p. 12). If you aren't sure if it's dry enough, try raising a corner of it off the texture sheet. If it holds together, peel off the resin and place it texture-side up on a flat surface and allow it to fully cure.

TIP Do NOT let the resin fully cure while on the texture sheet! It may bond to it, ruining the texture sheet.

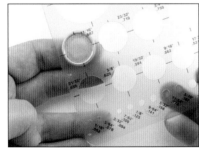

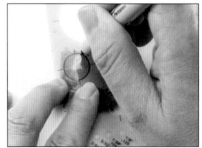

4 Use a circle guide to find a circle that best matches the circle bezel. Use a fine-tip permanent marker to trace the circle onto the smooth backside of the textured resin sheet.

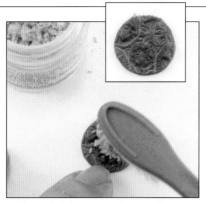

5 Depending on the thickness and rigidity of the resin, you can use scissors to cut out the circle and smooth the edges with sandpaper (see "Sanding," p. 13). Test-fit the textured resin circle by placing it into the bezel, and sand to adjust the fit as needed.

6 If you didn't use any dye on the texture sheet, or decide that the texture needs a little more pop, you can add some dry dye now. Dip an old toothbrush into a little bit of dye and, using a circular motion, scrub it into the recessed parts of the texture. Flip the pieces over, textured side down, and tap out any loose dye. Wipe any excess dye off the raised texture with a damp cloth.

7 Balance the ring: There are numerous ways to balance the ring bezel; use a third hand, tape to the table, use a bit of poster putty to stand it on the table, etc. I like using a medicine cup filled with dry rice. I find it stable, but easy enough to get the ring in and out with one hand, plus I can move the cup if I need a different angle, or just want to get it out of the way.

8 Use a toothpick to spread a light layer of resin on the bottom of the bezel. Place the textured resin circle in the bezel. Drive out any air bubbles with your fingers by pressing from the center of the textured circle out to the edges. Excess resin will bubble up between the texture and bezel; use a craft stick to spread the resin back over the top of the texture sheet. Wipe off any drips.

9 Check to see that the ring bezel is level. If needed, apply additional resin to the top of the texture sheet to create a smooth surface.

10 The dome height of the resin depends on the brand and viscosity of the resin. You can always add additional layers to build up the dome, or cover the texture that wasn't submerged with the first round of resin. Clean up any drips or overflow while wet. Make sure the bezel is level, and then cover and allow the resin to cure per manufacturer's instructions.

PROJECT 4
Window Earrings

One of my favorite scenes from "Ferris Bueller's Day Off" is when Ferris, Sloane, and Cameron visit The Art Institute of Chicago. Seeing so many masterpieces on film was breathtaking, but it was the scale and vivid colors from Marc Chagall's *America Windows* that stuck with me and inspired these earrings. Combining lightweight tissue paper with resin results in a translucent effect, making them even more Chagall-esque.

1 Tear a variety of strips and sections of gift wrap tissue paper.

2 Set a sheet of tissue paper on a plastic surface (see "Work Surface," p. 8). Use a sponge brush to apply a light coat of resin to the tissue paper, and place a fresh layer of tissue paper onto the wet resin. Alternate between colors of tissue paper and resin to build up 6–12 layers of paper.

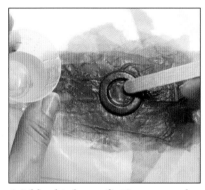

3 Firmly press a fiber washer into the layers of tissue paper; it will slightly sink and compress the layers of tissue paper.

4 Add a thin layer of resin to cover the tissue paper in the center of washer. Apply a thin, even coat of resin to the entire washer.

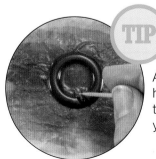

TIP

A toothpick is helpful for finalizing the placement of your model figure.

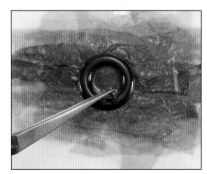

5 Use tweezers to gently place the seated model train figure on the rim of the washer.

6 Repeat steps 3–5 to make a second earring component.

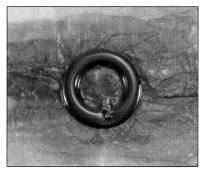

7 Cover and allow the resin to dry.

8 Use your fingernails to loosen the edges of the tissue paper away from the plastic. Gently peel the entire sheet away from the plastic.

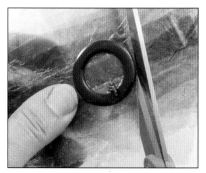

9 Use a scissors to carefully cut around the washer, taking care not to nick the washer. If necessary, you can refine the edges with sandpaper or sanding sticks (see "Sanding," p. 13).

10 You can stop here and your component will match the left component, or add a second coat of resin to fill the bezel of the washer and further adhere the seated figure to the component.

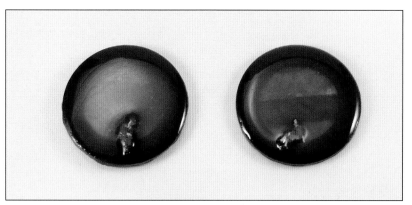

11 If necessary, cover and allow the pieces to cure. Refine any edges by sanding, if needed.

12 Use a permanent marker to mark the placement for the earring wires. Use your fingers to twist a small drill bit into the mark to create a divot for the drill (see "Drilling," p. 13).
13 Drill the components and attach an earring wire to each component with a jump ring (see "Jewelry Basics," p. 14).

HOW TO

PROJECT 5

Threaded Washers Bracelet

I get so many ideas for jewelry whenever I go to the hardware store. These fiber washers, also known as sheet gaskets, are inexpensive and come in a variety of sizes. Plus, a quick coat of resin instantly transforms these lightweight washers into bold, yet sleek, modern jewelry bezels.

WHAT YOU'LL NEED

Resin Component Supplies
- **5–6** fiber washers in 2 sizes (size determined by design; mine are ¾x.062 in./1.9x1.6cm and ⁷⁄₁₆x.062 in./1.1x1.6cm)
- Resin
- Resin dye
- Packaging tape
- Toothpicks
- Sponge brush or craft stick
- Black thread and scissors
- Sandpaper or sanding sticks
- Drill bits and drill

Jewelry Supplies
- **12–15** 8mm black jump rings
- **5–7** 8mm black jump rings
- **20–25** 8mm blue jump rings
- Lobster claw clasp
- **2** pairs chainnose pliers

1 Place a fiber washer on a piece of packaging tape. Burnish the tape with your finger to create a tight seal.

2 Add a few drops of clear resin inside the washer bezel.

To help keep the color of the components consistent, figure out how many washers are needed for the finished piece, and create all the components (and maybe a spare or two) at the same time.

3 Sticking to the edge of the bezel, apply a few drops of colored resin (see "Coloring Resin," p. 11). Use a toothpick to swirl the two resins together, keeping the clear resin at the center and graduating to the dark color around the edges.

If you over-mix, you can add in a drop of clear to the center of the bezel. It acts like a stone tossed into a pond and will push the tinted resin out like ripples. Just be sure not to fill the bezels to the top yet.

You can work from the entire spool of thread, or you may find it easier to cut off 1–2 ft. (30x61cm) sections and work with those.

4 Use a toothpick to press the end of the black thread into the resin. Use your fingers to gently guide the thread into rough circles around the bezel, while tacking the thread into place with the toothpick.

5 When you are satisfied with the circular pattern, trim the thread and tuck the end into the resin. You can add in a little more of the colored resin along the edge of the bezel. Cover and allow the resin to cure.

6 Once cured, removed the component from the tape. Remove any residue, if necessary. Use a sponge brush or craft stick to apply a thin coat of resin along the outside edge of the bezel. Place it on a plastic surface and apply a smooth solid coat of resin to the top. Cover and allow it to cure.

7 Flip the component over and apply a smooth coat of resin to the back. Cover and allow to cure.

8 Sand to refine any edges (see "Sanding," p. 13).

9 Use a permanent marker to mark the placement for the jump rings. Use your fingers to twist a small drill bit into the mark to create a divot for the drill (see "Drilling," p. 13).

10 Drill the components and connect with jump rings (see "Jewelry Basics," p. 14). I made five-jump ring chain mail rosettes using the blue jump rings and then connected the rosettes to the components with large black jump rings (see "Weaving Rosettes," right).

11 Use two small black jump rings to attach a clasp on one end, and attach alternating large and small black jump rings to make an extender chain on the other end.

WEAVING ROSETTES

Close one jump ring and open two rings of the same size. Thread an open jump ring through the center of a closed ring. Stack the rings one on top of the other. Adjust the direction of the top ring (shown in pink).

Thread a third ring (shown in purple) through the center of the two stacked rings. Adjust so the ring lays the same direction (clockwise) as the other rings. Any additional rings would be added in the same manner.

PROJECT 6

Spiral Ribbon Earrings

This is a fun way to incorporate a scrap of fabric or ribbon from a special outfit, or moment in time. But be sure to test your material first, since resin can darken some colors, or make light colors more transparent.

1 To prevent the ribbon from bonding with the wooden dowel, apply a smooth, even layer of packaging tape to the area of the wooden dowel you will use to wind the ribbon.

2 Use a sponge brush to apply a thin coat of resin to both sides of the ribbon. (You could also use strips of fabric in place of the ribbon.)

3 Secure one end of the ribbon to the tape-covered dowel rod by overlapping the ribbon or using tape or a rubber band.

4 Twist the ribbon down the length of the taped dowel while maintaining even spacing between the spirals of ribbon. Secure the opposite end of the ribbon to hold the spiral in place.

5 Allow the resin to cure. If the spiral is secure, you can stand the dowel in a box or flower vase; just make sure none of the wet resin drips or touches the stand. This will prevent resin from puddling or affecting the side in contact with your work surface.

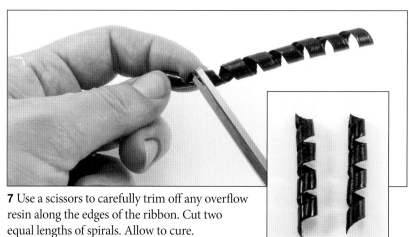

7 Use a scissors to carefully trim off any overflow resin along the edges of the ribbon. Cut two equal lengths of spirals. Allow to cure.

6 Once dry, gently pull the ribbon off the taped dowel.

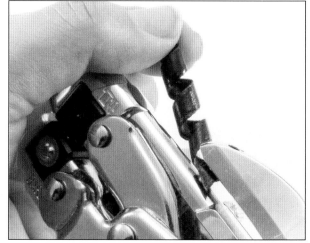

8 Use a permanent marker to mark where the holes will go. Use a small circle punch or scissors to make holes in both spirals.

9 Thread a jump ring through the spiral, the earring wire, and three short lengths of chain. Adjust the chains so they fall down the center of the spiral. Close the jump ring (see "Jewelry Basics," p. 14).
10 Repeat to make a second earring.

PROJECT 7

Pipe Bail Pendant

Copper pipe can be found in a multitude of diameters and lengths. I'm starting with a copper utility soft straight pipe, which is available in prepackaged 2-ft. (61cm) pieces. You may not be familiar with how simple it can be to cut copper pipes. A nifty gadget called a tube cutter is easy to operate, gives excellent results, and is inexpensive—the trifecta of reasons to introduce a new tool into the studio.

Make the Bail and Hanger

1 Use 80-grit sandpaper to sand the tube. This will roughen up the smooth surface and give it more tooth for the resin to adhere to.

2 Use a permanent marker and a ruler to mark 1¼ in. (3.2cm) from the end of the trimmed and sanded end of the tube.

 You may want to try a test-cut first, not only to acclimate yourself to a new tool, but also to compare the finished cut from the tool (slightly tapered) to the manufacturer's finished cut (straight).

3 Twist the knob at the base of the cutter to widen the space between the cutting wheel at the top of the tool and the rollers. Align the mark with the cutting wheel and turn the knob to close the gap and apply firm pressure. Don't over-tighten the knob, or you may crush the copper tube.

4 Revolve the tool 360 degrees around the tube. Notice the slight groove left by the cutting wheel? That is the start of the cut.

Most tube cutters come with a side reamer; it's the triangular piece that flips out like a pocket knife. The reamer is used to remove any burrs formed inside the tube. While I didn't need to use it for this project, if you cut up larger tubes or pipes (for backless bezels, for example), you might find it helpful to smooth out the inside of the cut pipe.

5 Give the knob a one-quarter to one-half twist to tighten, which will slowly press the cutting wheel further into the tube. Revolve the tool around the tube again. Repeat until the tube is cut.

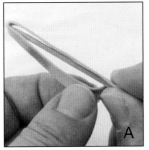
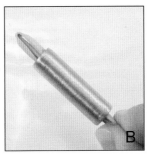
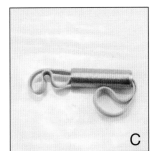

6 Use 80-grit sandpaper as needed to smooth the cut edge or refinish if the rollers left any marks on the tube.

7 Once the ribbon is twisted around the tube, it's helpful to have something to hold it in place so it doesn't unwind. You can strategically place silicone molds, use a silicone band, or lightly wrap a rubber band around the tube until the resin dries. Press a toothpick along the inside edge of a rubber band [**A**]. Thread the toothpick through the copper tube [**B**]. Remove the toothpick and adjust the rubber band so it's evenly distributed [**C**].

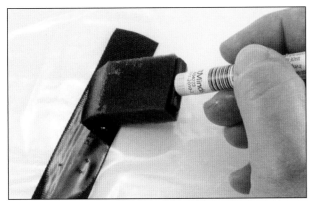

8 Use a sponge brush to apply a light coat of resin to both sides of a length of ribbon.

9 Place the copper tube onto the end of the ribbon. Using your fingers, snugly wrap the ribbon around the tube 2–4 times.

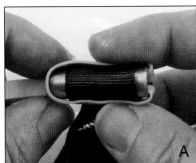

10 Place the wrapped tube and ribbon on a plastic work surface, and smooth the ribbon tail flat. Cover and allow the piece to dry. If you are using a rubber band, remove it before the component is completely dry to avoid it bonding with the ribbon (I waited about 3 hours). If the resin is still tacky, you can gently manipulate the ribbon to smooth any creases left by the rubber band. Cover and allow to cure.

If you are using the rubber band method, hold onto one end of the rubber band while flipping the other end over the tube and ribbon [**A**]. Then flip the opposite end of the rubber band over the tube and ribbon [**B**].

TIP

If your rubber band is too long, rather than wrap it around the component several times, tie a knot on one end of the rubber band (large enough so it can't be pulled through the tube), and only use the free end of the rubber band to secure the ribbon in place.

Create the Composite

11 Load a rubber stamp with colored ink. Wipe off any excess ink from the stamp with rubbing alcohol on a Q-tip. Stamp a few samples on white paper.

TIP

I wanted my ink colors to reflect the "tranquility" that this symbol represents, so to get a multi-color effect, I first loaded the stamp with a light color (teal). Then, rather than mashing the stamp into the ink pad, I flipped the stamp up to face me, and I sparingly dabbed darker colors (blue and purple) over the light teal color.

12 Since white paper will go slightly transparent when resin is applied (like water on white clothing), apply a light coat of white acrylic paint to the back side of the paper. Let the paint dry.

13 Use a scissors or a paper punch to cut out the stamp. Cut additional paper to create a composite.

14 Use a glue stick to adhere the layers together. Use plenty of glue to compress and burnish the layers together to drive out any trapped air bubbles. Allow to dry.

15 Apply a layer of resin to completely coat the top of the composite. Use your craft stick to further burnish the layers and drive out any trapped air bubbles. Cover and allow to cure.

16 If you do find an air bubble in your cured piece, you can pop it with a pin or toothpick. Lightly wet sand with 400-grit to remove any ridges from the bubble (see "Sanding," p. 13).

TIP

Only sand enough to make the area around the bubble flush with the rest of the component. The indentation left from the air bubble will fill in with fresh resin. If you over-sand, you risk sanding into your paper components and altering those as well.

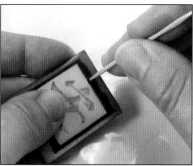

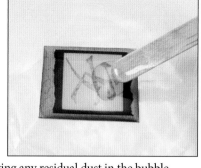

17 Clean and dry the component, removing any residual dust in the bubble indentation with a pin or toothpick. Apply a final coat of resin, cover, and allow to cure.

18 Determine final placement of the composite on the ribbon hanger, and use a scissors to trim the ribbon.

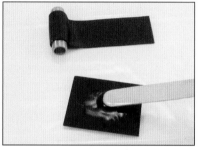

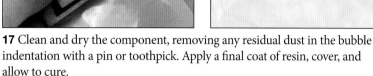

19 Apply a light coat of resin to the back of the composite. Firmly press the composite onto the ribbon, driving out any air bubbles with your fingers. Set down, front facing up, on a flat surface, check final alignment of the composite, and then cover and allow to cure.

20 Once cured, you can flip the pendant over and stabilize so it is level (I'm using silicone rings). Apply a coat of resin to the back of the composite and the ribbon. Cover and allow to cure.

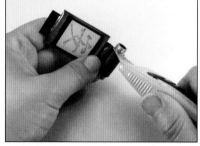

21 If you have any overflow resin on the pipe, carefully press a craft or utility knife along the edge of the ribbon, down to the pipe. The resin can be peeled off of the pipe.

22 String the pendant on a chain or beaded strand.

PROJECT 8
Stir Stick
Necklace

Try your hand at elevating the humble paint stick into a truly remarkable statement necklace. This hefty piece is a great example of the beauty of asymmetry. You can achieve the right balance with careful placement of chain and focal components.

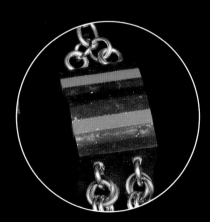

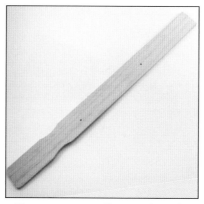

1 Use a saw to cut off a 4-in. (10cm) section from a paint stir stick.

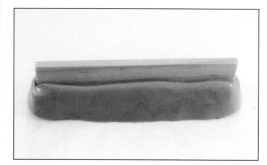

2 Use molding compound to make a mold of the rectangular piece of wood (see "Resin Techniques," p. 10).

3 After the molding compound is set up, remove the piece of wood. Fill the mold with dyed resin (see "Coloring Resin," p. 11). Cover and allow the resin to dry.

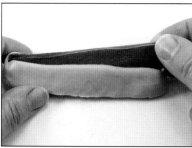

4 Remove the resin from the mold. Set it on a flat surface to cure.

5 Repeat steps 3 and 4 to create three more colored resin pieces.

6 Use a saw to cut the cured slats of resin into 2-in. (5cm) sections.

7 Test-fit the resin slats by stacking them and checking for gaps. If needed, trim or sand any overflow to ensure the slats stack snugly.

8 Use a sponge brush to apply a thin coat of resin on one side of a slat. Firmly press the second slat onto the wet resin, and apply a thin coat of resin onto the second slat. Continue alternating between the coats of resin and the slats until the entire slab is assembled.

9 Lay the slab onto a heavy plastic sheet or bag and tightly wrap the plastic around the slab, compressing the slats. For extra compression, clamp the slab and allow the resin to dry.

12 Once you have the shape you like, continue sanding while running up to 1000-grit sandpaper (see "Sanding," p. 13).

10 Once dry, unwrap the resin and allow the slab to cure.

11 After the slab is fully cured and bonded, you can cut, shape, and sand it as you would a solid piece of resin. Use 80-grit sandpaper to smooth all sides of the slab. Continue using the rough grit to add a beveled edge to the front of the slab.

TIP

I found it helpful to rinse the components between sandpaper grits. Also, a soft-bristled toothbrush is helpful for removing dust from small gaps or air bubbles that are exposed during the sanding procedure.

13 Using a saw, cut the slab into two equal halves. Sand to refine and smooth the cut edges.

TIP I used my wood saw and miter box to cut the component in half. If you have a finer saw blade, or even a jeweler's saw, you would have less sanding to remove the saw blade marks.

TIP The pilot holes don't need to be as long as the screw, but they do need to be drilled straight into the resin. If you come in at an angle, the eye won't sit properly and the screw may tear through the side of the component.

14 Use a ruler and permanent marker to mark four drill holes for the screw eye placement. Create a divot by pressing a drill bit into the resin and twisting between your fingers. Repeat on the second component.

15 Using the divots as a guide, select a drill bit smaller than the screw eye post and drill pilot holes into the resin.

16 Use your fingers to twist the screw eyes into the pilot holes. Repeat for the second component.

17 The lengths of the chain are up to your individual preference, so adjust accordingly. To finish the necklace: Use two jump rings to attach a 16-in. (41cm) piece of chain to the tapered end of a component (see "Jewelry Basics," p. 14). Repeat to attach the second component on the other end of the chain.

18 Use jump rings in a pattern as desired to attach two chains (11½ in./ 29.2cm and 9½ in./24.1cm) to the outside screw eye. Use a jump ring pattern to attach a 6-in. (15cm) chain to the inside screw eye. I added orange rosettes to one component and blue rosettes to the second component. See "Weaving Rosettes," p. 33, to create a rosette.

18 Use a the same jump ring patterns to attach the chains to the second set of screw eyes on the other component. Attach the 6-in. (15cm) chain to the inside screw eye, and the other two chains to the outside screw eye. Swapping the chains adds a twist to the traditional swag pattern of the chains.

PROJECT 9

Retro Targets Pendant

Create numerous bull's-eyes all in one compact pendant. Attach to a premade chain or neck cord, or create your own complementary chain. This application can get pretty messy, so it's best to use plastic over wax paper on your work surface.

Resin Component Supplies
- Colored paper, 2–6 colors
- Scissors
- Resin
- Saw and miter box
- Drill with a variety of drill bits
- Sandpaper and toothbrush
- Permanent marker and ruler
- Sponge brush and craft stick

Jewelry Supplies
- **3** large jump rings
- Finished neck chain of your choice
- **2** pairs chainnose pliers

MAKING A BRICK

Choose two or more colors of paper. I like to vary between bright and dark colors to create high contrast. Cut the paper to roughly the same size, I cut each letter-sized sheet into fourths. Just remember: Whatever size you cut the paper, will you have a way to finish cutting it? Will it fit into your miter box, or will you need an alternate plan to cut the brick? Then stack the paper into the order it should appear in the brick. The paper thickness and number of colors will determine how many sheets of paper you will need. I made my finished brick about ¼ in. (6mm) thick.

1 Use resin and paper to make a multi-colored brick (see "Making a Brick").

 If you'd like one layer to appear thicker, use multiple sheets of that same color. For example, 1 sheet of blue, 1 sheet of black, 2 or 3 sheets of orange, and repeat the pattern.

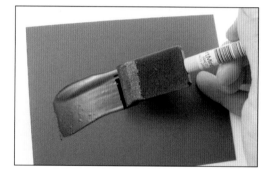

2 Use a sponge brush to apply a coat of resin to the first sheet of paper in the stack.

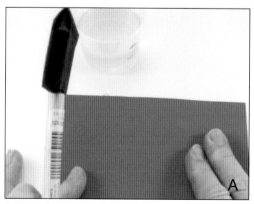

A

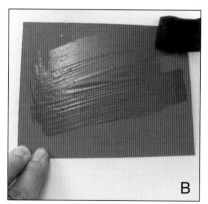

B

3 Place the second sheet of paper in the stack over the resin. Press from the center of the sheet out to the edges to drive out any trapped air bubbles [**A**]. Then apply a coat of resin to the second sheet [**B**].

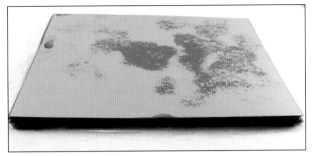

 TIP The amount of resin will vary depending on the weight and type of paper used. Heavy or shiny-finished paper may need extra time to let the resin "soak into" the paper (like the blue spots on the sample to the right) before moving to the next step. If there isn't enough resin, or it doesn't fully saturate the paper, the brick will peel apart.

4 Repeat coating and stacking the paper until you are satisfied with the height of the brick. For reference, the brick pictured is roughly 24 sheets high.

5 Wrap the brick in plastic. A large zip-top bag works great for this. Add some weight on top to compress the brick (I like to use several large, heavy books), and allow the brick to dry (see "Dry Time vs. Cure Time," p. 12).

6 Once the resin is dry (see your resin manufacturer's instructions for recommended drying time), unwrap the brick and remove it from the plastic. Allow the resin to cure, and depending on the thickness and amount of resin used, you may want to wait an extra day or two before trying to cut the brick, to insure all the resin has fully cured.

7 Cut your component. Using your miter box and saw, cut your pendant into a rough rectangle and add a beveled edge to the bottom edge (see "Using a Miter Box," p. 13). Sand the edges smooth and level, working from 80–400-grit sandpaper (see "Sanding," p. 13).

8 Use a variety of drill bit sizes in a power drill or rotary tool to cut out divots. Apply light pressure and go slowly, straight down; you only want to cut the first few layers of paper, not go all the way through the stack.

 TIP

By compressing the brick, you are insuring a tighter bond between the pages; however, this also means whatever you set on top of the brick can leave an impression in the soggy paper. For best results, press the brick between two flat surfaces, and make sure any additional weight is evenly distributed across the entire brick.

 **TIP**

Practice drilling on a scrap bit of brick before attempting it on your cut and sanded component.

9 Once you have all your divots in place, there will likely be a fuzzy buildup of extra paper around the edges of each divot. Flip the pendant, face down, onto 400-grit wet sandpaper and lightly sand off the excess paper. If you sand too much, you will go through your top layer of paper. Rinse clean under running water. If needed, use an old toothbrush to clean out the divots and remove all the dust buildup.

10 Dry the component. Add a layer of resin. Start by filling the divots, removing any air bubbles, and then gently smoothing the resin across the top of the component. Use a sponge brush or your finger to add a thin coat of resin to seal the edges of the component. Cover and allow to cure.

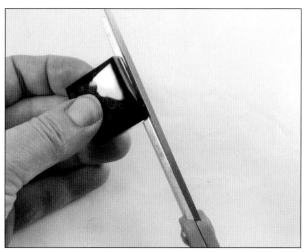 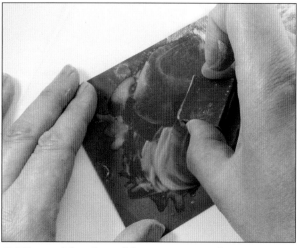

11 Use scissors to trim any excess resin from the pendant.

12 Wet-sand the edges of the component with 800-grit to smooth the resin.

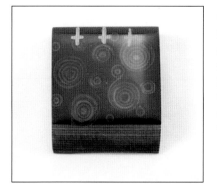

13 Staying at least ⅛ in. (3mm) from the edge, use a permanent marker and a ruler to mark placement for drill holes. Use a small drill bit to drill holes in the pendant.
14 Add jump rings, and string on a finished chain of your choice (see "Jewelry Basics," p. 14).

PROJECT 10

Glowing Filigree Bracelet

While working with bezels can be convenient, sometimes it's hard to find one in the size you need. Luckily, with a little patience and some cardstock, you can create a custom-size "rimless bezel" to complement any shape and size filigree component.

WHAT YOU'LL NEED

Resin Component Supplies
- Cardstock or heavy paper
- Prefabricated filigree component
- Pencil and permanent marker
- Scissors
- Resin
- Triple Glow Powder
- Drill and drill bits
- Sandpaper or sanding sticks

Jewelry Supplies
- **2** 3-in. (7.6cm) pieces of chain
- **3** jump rings
- Lobster claw clasp
- Chainnose and/or bentnose pliers

1 Place a filigree component onto white cardstock or heavy paper. Use a pencil to trace the outline of the filigree component onto the paper, leaving an approximately ⅛-in. border. Cut out the shape.

2 Mix the resin. Use Triple Glow Powder to dye the wet resin (see "Coloring Resin," p. 11). Apply a coat of resin to the paper. Cover and allow to cure.

3 Flip the paper over. Apply a second coat of glow-in-the-dark resin to the other side. Cover and allow to cure.

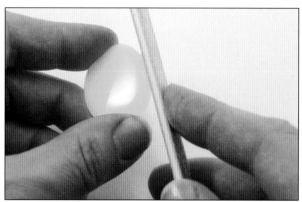

4 Determine which side is the front and which is the back—you may want to test the glow strength to determine which looks better with your filigree. Once determined, hold the filigree in place above the resin and check if the border is even. Use sandpaper to refine the edges.

TIP Sanding sticks or emery boards (yep, the same kind you use for your fingernails) are handy substitutes for sheets of sandpaper when you are working in tight spaces or for projects needing minimal sanding.

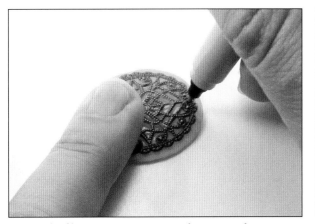

5 Place the filigree component over the resin and use a fine-point permanent marker to mark the drill hole on one end (see "Drilling," p. 13). Drill the hole and run a jump ring through the resin and filigree to secure the two pieces together (see "Jewelry Basics," p. 14).

6 Depending on your filigree, and how your finished component will be used, you may need to secure the pieces in more than one place. To help maintain alignment between the two components, mark, drill, and secure one point at a time.

7 Finish the bracelet: Connect a piece of fancy chain to each jump ring. (I made my own chain with jump ring rosettes; see "Weaving Rosettes," p. 33.) Add a clasp to one end of the bracelet with a jump ring.

DESIGN OPTION

Use permanent markers, acrylic paint, or even stamps to create your own glow-in-the-dark patterns instead of using prefabricated filigree components. You can also send a "secret message!" Match your glow and ink/paint colors, so your message or pattern will only be illuminated in the dark.

PROJECT 11

Spacescape Cuff

"Star Wars" was the first movie to capture my imagination with the majestic beauty and boundless possibilities of space. Then came "Star Trek," which eventually led to "Firefly." Today, a constant stream of Twitter and Instagram accounts from space agencies, and astronauts posting images from the International Space Station help satiate my hunger for spacescapes. So really, it's no wonder that when I saw glow-in-the-dark powdered dye, it instantly inspired me to try and recreate the beauty of space, without the worry of The Borg or Reaver interference.

1 Use a scissors to cut approximately 8–9 in. (20–23cm) of ribbon.

If you need spacescape inspiration, get online and look up "Hubble Telescope images," or "nebula gas cloud."

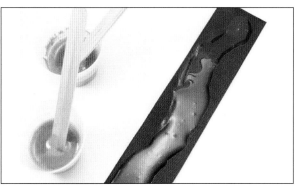

2 Mix a small batch of resin. Divide and color small amounts of blue, purple, yellow, and red using the Triple Glow Powder (see "Coloring Resin," p. 11). Drizzle a wavy row of yellow along the length of the ribbon.

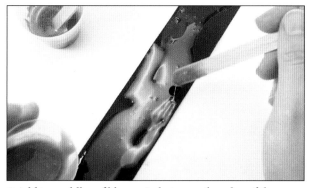

3 Add in puddles of blue resin between the edge of the ribbon and the yellow resin.

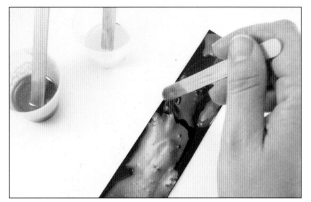

4 Drizzle purple dyed resin between the blue and yellow resin. Add some red along the edges of the purple.

5 Use a toothpick to lightly swirl the colors together.

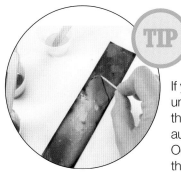

TIP

If you are working under a bright light, the glow powder will automatically charge. Occasionally snap off the lights to check and refine your glow colors.

6 Once you are satisfied with your swirls, add in the "stars." Use your fingers to lightly sprinkle a small amount of the yellow glow powder over the wet resin. Sprinkle heavier amounts of powder to create star clusters.

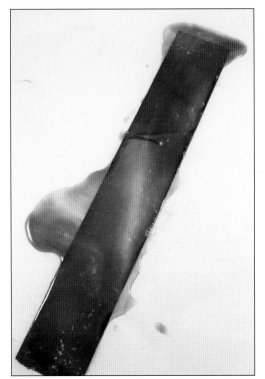

7 Don't worry about overflow; cover and allow the resin to dry (see "Dry Time vs. Cure Time," p. 12).

8 Use a scissors to trim the overflow resin from the ribbon. The ribbon should maintain a fair amount of flexibility, even with the dried resin (as shown in the top photo). At this point, it is a personal preference if you feel an additional layer of resin is needed. Don't forget to dust another top layer of "stars." Cover and allow the resin to dry.

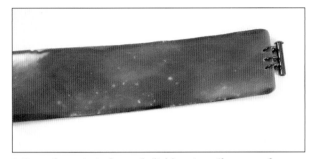

9 Once the resin is dry and pliable, trim off any overflow, and cut the length to fit your wrist, while rounding off the edges. Mark and drill or punch holes along one side of the ribbon for the clasp. Attach the clasp using jump rings (see "Jewelry Basics," p. 14).

10 Butt the ends of the bracelet together to align the holes.

11 Drill holes and use jump rings to attach the second half of the clasp to the other end of the ribbon.

12 Set up the bracelet to cure into its final shape. If it cures flat, it may not be pliable enough to wrap around your wrist. If that is the case, try submerging the resin ribbon in hot water from the tap (not boiling). The warm water will soften the resin, allowing it to be gently reshaped without being damaged. While the resin is pliable, wrap it around a bracelet mandrel, rolling pin, or other makeshift wrist-shaped object (like my dowels with a clothes pin to mimic the contour of a wrist) to cool and cure into its final shape.

PROJECT 12
Quilled Disk Earrings

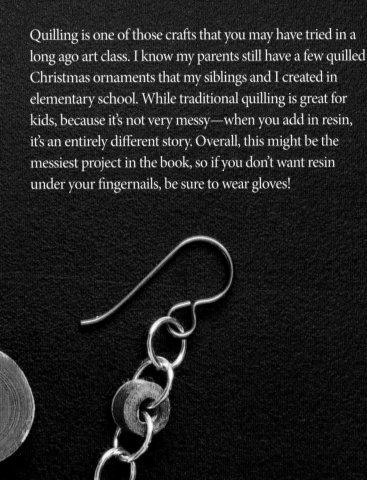

Quilling is one of those crafts that you may have tried in a long ago art class. I know my parents still have a few quilled Christmas ornaments that my siblings and I created in elementary school. While traditional quilling is great for kids, because it's not very messy—when you add in resin, it's an entirely different story. Overall, this might be the messiest project in the book, so if you don't want resin under your fingernails, be sure to wear gloves!

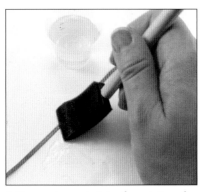

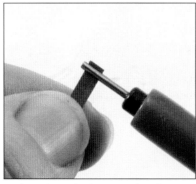

1 Use a scissors to trim four strips of quilling paper (two of color A and two of color B) the same length. Use a sponge brush to apply a light coat of resin along the entire length of a strip of color A (pink) and color B (blue) quilling paper.

2 Place the end of a strip of quilling paper into the slot of a quilling tool.

3 While maintaining a light tension on the quilling paper with your non-dominant hand, spin the quilling tool as if you are winding a watch with your dominant hand. The paper will begin to coil upon itself. Use your fingers on your non-dominant hand to keep the layers evenly aligned.

4 Add in the second color. When color A has a tail 2–3 in. (5–7.6cm) long, stop spinning the tool. Place the end of the color B strip (shown in blue) between the disk and the tail. Use your fingers to align the two colors, and then continue to spin the tool to wind up the disk.

5 After all the paper is coiled, continue spinning the disk between your fingers to compress and tighten the paper together.

6 Wiggle the quilling tool to loosen the disk, and remove.

7 Cover the disk and allow it to cure. If you find that the end of the disk won't stick and starts to uncoil, gently set the disk next to a silicone mold with the tail pressed up against the mold. (Some especially uncooperative disks may need to be trapped between two silicone molds to prevent uncoiling.) Be sure not to press them so close that the disk distorts.

8 Repeat to coil a second matching disk. You can also coil additional small disks of either color if you wish to add them to your earrings. I coiled one length of color A for each small disk.

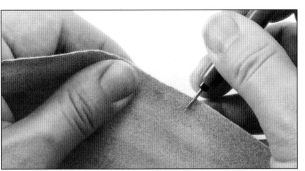

9 Periodically check your quilling tool and remove any wet resin. When you are done with your disks, clean out your quilling tool immediately! The narrow opening can easily be filled in with drying resin, ruining your tool. Wipe off the wet resin with baby wipes and run heavy cardstock through the gap. If you are unable to get cardstock through, you can use a sheet of 120–220-grit sandpaper instead. Thread as much of the sandpaper in as you can, and using a sawing motion, drag the tool back and forth to remove any dried resin. Rotate the tool around to sand both sides.

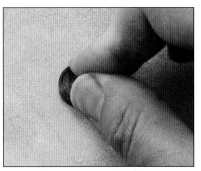

10 After the coils dry, sand (80–400-grit) the face and back of the disks to a smooth finish (see "Sanding," p. 13). If there are any obvious drips or ridges along the edges, remove those with sandpaper as well.

DESIGN OPTION

If you prefer a high-gloss resin finish, sand until you have a flat surface, clean off all the dust, and apply a light domed layer of resin. Cover, and allow the resin to cure.

11 Once the surfaces have been sanded and cleaned, or cured to the final finish, use a permanent marker to mark drill holes for the jump rings. Use a drill bit and drill to drill the holes (see "Drilling," p. 13).

12 Use jump rings to connect a large and small disk as shown (see "Jewelry Basics," p. 14), and add an earring wire to the end. Repeat to make a second earring.

PROJECT 13

Quilled Asymmetrical Necklace

Quilling disks are a fun way to add a splash of color to a project. But I think it's even more interesting to see only part of a disk being used in a project. Only using one half also gives you a backup in case something goes sideways (sometimes literally) while drilling the holes.

1 Start with a cured and sanded disk of quilling paper (see "Quilled Disk Earrings," p. 59 for instructions). Figure out which side you'd like as the front and add another domed layer of resin. Cover and allow to cure. Prepare two additional accent disks to complete the asymmetrical necklace.

TIP Because of the thin profile of the disk and the difficulty that can occur while drilling, you may find it helpful to prepare several disks to use as backups or practice dummies.

2 Use a jeweler's saw, coping saw, or other thin-bladed saw to cut through the center of the disk. While using a bench pin would be easiest, it is possible to use a corner of scrap wood as a cutting surface. Hold the disk in place with a thumb on one side of the blade, and a finger on the other. Press the disk down into the wood; if you try to press the disk together, you'll bind up the saw and make it much harder to cut, and you could potentially break a thin blade.

TIP While your miter box and saw may work, its rough teeth and wide blade could leave your disk in shambles. The thinner the blade, the less of the disk you'll lose during the cutting process.

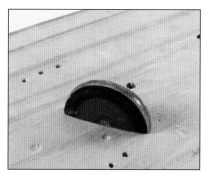

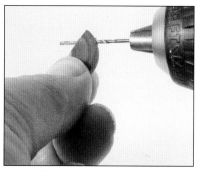

3 Sand the cut surface smooth and even, running through 120–400-grit.

4 The thin profile of the disk will make this next step tricky, but remember there is a second half of the disk as backup, just in case. To help guide the drill bit to the correct placement, press a slightly larger bit onto the disk and twist it with your fingers while pressing down. This will leave a slight divot for the drill bit.

5 Hold the cut edge of the disk firmly against a piece of scrap wood. Place the bit into the divot and drill straight through the disk at a slight angle. (The drill bit shows the entrance and exit points.)

6 Repeat to drill the opposite end of the half circle.

You can also drill halfway through the disk, and then estimate the drill trajectory and exit point. Then drill from the estimated exit and try to meet halfway. For me, trying to hold the disk steady along that dome usually resulted in uneven holes.

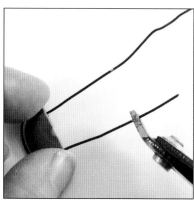

7 You can widen the drilled hole to accommodate jump rings as in the first photo, but sometimes getting that angle to accommodate the curve of a jump ring can be tricky. So, I generally prefer to use wire instead, as in the second photo. Gently bend the wire into a U-shape and slide the ends through the drilled holes on either end of the domed half of the disk.

8 Use wire cutters to trim the ends to about 1 in. (2.5cm) long.

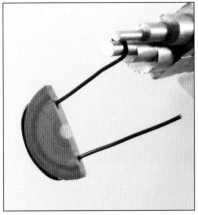

9 Use a roundnose pliers or stepped mandrel pliers to roll up each wire end until it is flush with the half disk.

10 Drill the two additional accent disks. Although you can drill them across the diameter through the thin side, I chose a button-hole style for mine.

11 Use coordinating jump rings to attach the chain to either end of the half disk. Lay out the accent disks (with coordinating jump rings) to determine placement.

12 Depending on your chain, cut or open the links to add the first accent disk with coordinating jump rings (see "Jewelry Basics," p. 14).

13 For a symmetrical necklace, add the second accent disk on the opposite side of the half disk focal. For an asymmetrical necklace, add the second accent disk to the same side as the first.

14 Adjust the length of the chain and add a clasp to one end with a jump ring.

PROJECT 14

Inlay Pendant

Now that you've seen how to make a simple two-color disk, it's time to kick it up a notch. Using the same method from the "Quilled Disk Earrings," p. 57, combine a few more colors or strands of quilling paper to make a larger disk, at least 1 in. (2.5cm) in diameter. The larger you make this disk, the easier it will be to inlay the small disks.

1 Start with a cured and sanded disk of quilling paper (see "Quilled Disk Earrings," p. 57, for instructions).

2 Use a permanent marker to mark several locations to drill holes for inlay.

WHAT YOU'LL NEED

Resin Component Supplies
- Quilling paper in your choice of colors
- Quilling tool
- Resin
- Sponge brush and craft stick
- Sandpaper
- Drill/drill bits
- Permanent marker

Jewelry Supplies
- **1** jump ring
- **2** pairs chainnose pliers

3 Use a drill bit and power drill or rotary tool to drill holes for inlay (see "Drilling," p. 13). Use a variety of sizes; the larger the hole, the easier it will be to inlay. When drilling larger holes, start with a small bit and then redrill the hole with a slightly larger bit, until you get to the final size.

TIP To help maintain the structural integrity of the disk, evenly space the holes for the inlays and stay at least 1/8 in. (3mm) away from the edge.

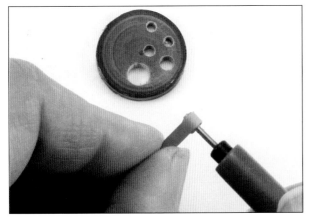

4 Because the size of the inlay will vary, it's best to do a dry test-fit first. Use a quilling tool to coil a dry strip of quilling paper into a disk. Periodically hold the disk to the hole to eyeball the fit. Once the coil is approximately the correct size, trim the paper and place it into the inlay hole. Continue until all the inlays are filled.

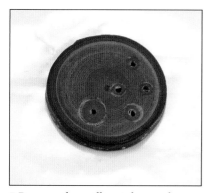

5 Remove the quilling inlays and uncoil the paper. Use a sponge brush to apply resin to the strip. Use the quilling tool to re-coil, and place the inlay back into the disk. Press the inlays so they are as level as possible with the disk. Cover and allow the disks to cure.

6 Once cured, the inlays may not be perfectly flush with the rest of the disk. Use 120–800-grit sandpaper to smooth the face of the disk. Use running water to rinse all the dust and sanding sludge from the disk.

7 Determine your final finish. You can either leave the disk as is, or if you prefer a domed, high-gloss finish, add a final layer of resin. Cover and allow it to cure.

8 Drill, add a jump ring (see "Jewelry Basics," p. 14), and string as desired.

PROJECT 15
Bird Pendant

I love home remodeling. A fresh coat of paint or a newly refinished
floor really makes me happy. However, the downside is my "collection
of project ideas." Sure Pinterest helps, er ... enables, but there is nothing
like having physical paint chips when figuring out new décor. After the
project is finished, it seems like a waste to toss out potentially interesting
jewelry backgrounds—so I discovered a new use for them instead.

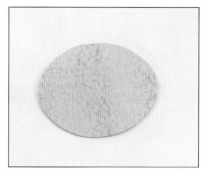

1 Cut or punch out an oval shape from your paint chip or sheet of heavy scrapbook paper.

TIP If you find a paint color you really like, rather than swiping the entire catalog of paint chips from your local store, many stores sell paint samples that are only a few ounces—which would be more than enough to make dozens of your own paint chips.

2 Apply a thin coat of clear resin to the front of your oval.

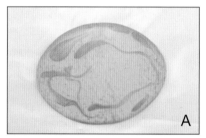

3 Pour a small amount of clear resin into a new measuring cup and add dye "see "Coloring Resin," p. 11). Use a toothpick to drizzle tinted resin along the outer edge of the oval. Use the toothpick to swirl the colored resin into the clear resin [**A, B**]. Cover and allow to cure.

4 Use a paintbrush and black acrylic paint to cover any writing on the back of the paint chip. Set it aside to dry.

TIP Once the paint is dry, check the front for any stray paint marks. Since acrylic is a water-based paint, it can be wiped off the resin with a little water on a soft cloth, or you can easily scrape it off with your fingernail without damaging the resin.

5 Cover the back of the oval with a coat of resin. You can leave it clear, or swirl in coordinating colored resin with a toothpick. It's good practice, and if you don't like it after it cures, you can paint over it and try again. Cover and allow the resin to cure.

6 Work on the front of the component next. I like to choose images that will be painted in two layers, but plan as many layers as you like. For this piece, the branch will be further away than the birds. Use a small paintbrush and black acrylic paint to add a branch across the oval. Let the paint dry.

TIP

Remember, acrylic paint is water-based. If you don't like your background, wipe it off with water and a soft cloth and try again.

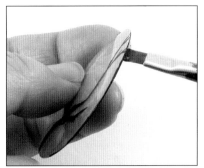
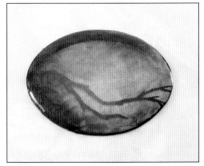

7 Using the side of your paintbrush, apply a thin coat of black acrylic paint around the edge of the oval, and let it dry.

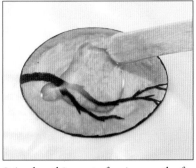
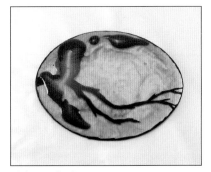

8 Apply a thin coat of resin over the front of the oval. If you want to create a vignette effect, add some darker resin along the edge of the oval (I'm using a metallic brown), and swirl it into the clear resin.

TIP

The paint could still be easily scratched off, so use a light touch when using any craft sticks or toothpicks to apply resin.

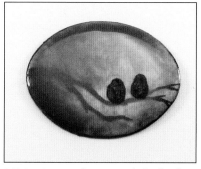  

9 Paint in your foreground: the birds. Break the birds down into simple shapes. The body is an oval and the head is a circle that overlaps the oval. It's kind of a figure-8 that's been squished. Paint in rough triangles for tails and let the paint dry.

10 If needed, once the paint is dry, use a toothpick to scrape or refine your bird shapes. The toothpick point will gently scrape away the paint without damaging the resin underneath. Blow or wipe away any stray paint flecks.

11 Apply a coat of clear resin to the top of the component. You can stop here or bring out the background color, in this case metallic gold, with a few drops of colored resin. Swirl it into the clear resin, sticking mostly to the inner part of the oval.

12 Because the brown was a little heavy, it covers most of the blue around the edge. I'm just adding in a few drops to swirls along the perimeter of the oval, keeping away from the gold to avoid mixing the colors.

 TIP If you are concerned about the colors mixing, allow the previous layer of resin to dry, and then apply an additional layer of clear resin and swirl in your second color.

13 Cover and allow the resin to cure. Use a drill bit and drill to add holes for jump rings (see "Drilling," p. 13).

14 Finish the pendant: Attach a jump ring to each hole (see "Jewelry Basics," p. 14). Attach chain and bead dangles as desired.

PROJECT 16

Stained Glass Pendant

While I do enjoy creating stained glass creations, the medium can be a bit cumbersome for jewelry. Use resin to replicate the look of leaded stained glass.

WHAT YOU'LL NEED

Resin Component Supplies
- Toothpicks and scissors
- Resin and resin dye
- Black permanent marker
- Craft knife or saw
- White glue and packaging tape
- Craft knife or sandpaper (optional)
- Drill/drill bit

Jewelry Supplies
- **2** jump rings
- 24 in. (61cm) fancy chain
- **2** pairs chainnose pliers

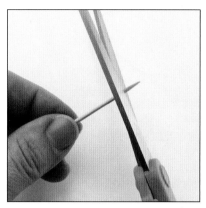

1 Use a scissors to trim one pointed end off of six toothpicks.

2 Use a permanent marker to color the toothpicks black. Allow them to dry thoroughly, or the marker dye may bleed into the wet resin.

TIP You can use acrylic paint in place of a permanent marker and get the same results.

3 Slightly overlap two strips of packaging tape. Place the sheet of tape sticky side up on the table. Arrange the toothpicks in an overlapping V-shape with the cut ends running down the center. You may need to adjust the angle of the cut ends so they lay flush with the other toothpicks. Be sure to re-color any trimmed ends.

4 Once you have all the toothpicks in place, get the ends as snug as possible. To prevent the resin from spilling out through the gaps, use a bit of Elmer's school glue on a toothpick to fill in any gaps and allow it to dry.

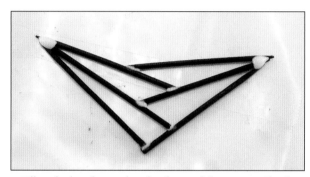

5 Fill each chamber with a thin layer of clear resin. Check for any leakage. If the resin does leak at this point, allow the clear layer to dry and fill in any gaps. Then apply a second thin layer of resin.

6 Mix your choice of colored resin (see "Coloring Resin," p. 11). Use a toothpick to add a few drops of colored resin into the wet clear resin. Drag the toothpick through the drops to swirl the colored resin into the clear.

7 Once you have the colors swirled to your satisfaction, cover and allow the resin cure.

8 After the resin is cured, carefully and slowly remove the packaging tape. If there is any overflow, you can trim it off with a scissors. If it is too thick for a scissors, you may need a craft knife, or saw and sandpaper (see "Sanding," p. 13).

9 If the chambers of resin are concave after curing, add another layer of clear resin to the top for added stability. Clean up any wet resin, cover, and allow it to cure.

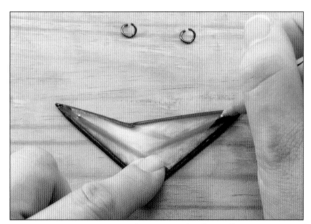

10 Use a permanent marker to mark where the jump rings for the chain will go. With the resin component on a piece of scrap wood, drill the holes with a drill bit and power drill, or other rotary tool.

11 Thread a jump ring through one hole. I chose to skip a clasp and instead attached a long chain that would fit over my head to the jump ring (see "Jewelry Basics," p. 14). Repeat on the other side of the pendant.

PROJECT 17

Lath Pendant

One of the charming, and sometimes challenging, aspects of owning an old home is fixing or maintaining the lath-and-plaster walls. Most older homes use thin strips of horizontally hung wood, called lath. These parallel rows of lath form the support structure for the plaster overlay. It's still pretty common to find lath at your local hardware store. If you look closely (or ask) there is usually a bin of "rejected" wood. While most builders try to avoid organic inclusions (knots, overlapping branches, bark, etc.), this is exactly the sort of thing you want to focus on for this project.

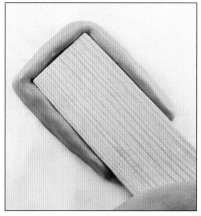

1 Use some molding compound and a squared off piece of lath to make a mold (see "Using Two-Part Silicone Molding Compound," p. 10).

2 Find a section of lath with an interesting inclusion. (I chose to work with two pieces so I could pick the best option for my final pendant.) Carefully look over both sides of the lath for places where branches (top lath) or bark (lower lath) became part of the lath. These sections can usually be removed or broken away by hand.

3 Place the lath into the resin mold. Although lath has a universal width, you may find that you need to customize the fit just a little. Use extra wooden craft sticks to shim the lath to lay level in the mold. If needed, a little bit of packaging tape can be used to snug up the opening of the mold around the wood.

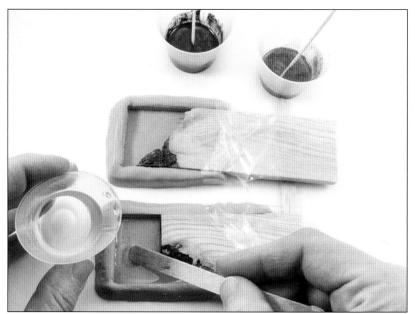

4 Mix up a batch of clear resin and two colors (I'm using brown and pink) (see "Coloring Resin," p. 11). Add a thin layer of clear resin to the mold.

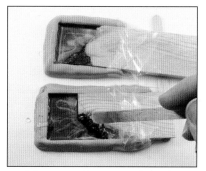

5 Drip a few drops of the lighter-colored resin into the clear, and swirl to create a marbling effect.

6 Add a few drops of the darker-colored resin along the edge furthest from the lath. Swirl the dark resin into the far edge of the resin, extending a few tendrils up toward the lath.

7 Add in more clear resin along the edge of the lath, and drizzle the clear to break up and thin out the colors.

Remember, you want to be able to see the natural details of the wood, so add enough clear resin to accomplish that.

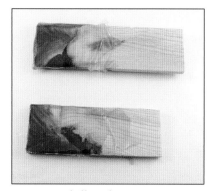

8 Cover and allow the resin to cure.
9 Once cured, remove the packaging tape (if used) and remove the piece from the mold. You may notice ridges from the tape, and texture on the back from the mold. Don't worry about either of those things yet; eventually, they will be sanded or cut off.

10 Plan the shape of your pendant. Use painters tape, paper, or (my favorite) Post-It Notes to lay out your final shape.

You will need to plan where and how the bail will be placed, and sanding may reduce the cut component's size slightly.

11 Use your saw and miter box to cut out your pendant (see "Using a Miter Box," p. 13). I try to keep my cuts to a minimum and salvage cut-offs for additional components.

12 Sand all the sides of the pendant. For this piece, I sanded the front to 400-grit and all sides and back up to 800-grit (see "Sanding," p. 13). I also slightly rounded off the edges.

13 Rather than leaving a plain hole for the jump ring bail, dress it up with an eyelet. Find a drill bit that is the same size as your eyelet and drill a hole.

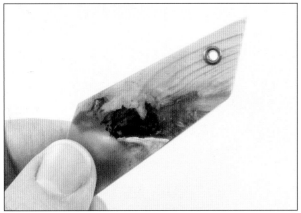

14 Apply a thin layer of resin with a sponge brush to the lath component and push the eyelet in place. Depending on how much sanding you did, you may also have exposed raw wood. Apply a thin coat of resin to protect the wood. If you coat the entire pendant at one time, you need to suspend it to dry. You can use a long needle or length of wire and a third hand, or thread a piece of fishing line through the hole and tape/secure between two upside-down glasses.

15 Once cured, decide if you are happy with the finish. I did one light round of sanding on the sides and back from 400–800-grit sandpaper. Remember, you just want to smooth out the surface, not remove the layer of resin. I also added one final coat of resin to the top, sealing the eyelet in place and giving the front of the pendant a high-gloss finish.

16 Finish the pendant: Add a jump ring (see "Jewelry Basics," p. 14), and string on a finished chain.

TIP Avoid getting wet resin in the eyelet hole, or you will need to drill it out after it is cured.

PROJECT 18
Half-Circle Earrings

I love the smell of fresh-cut wood. For me, it's a signal that there is some sort of transformation occurring. Whether it's building a new piece of furniture or a new jewelry component, they both smack of the anticipation of creativity.

1 Use your saw and miter box to cut a ¼-in. (6mm) section from the dowel (see "Using a Miter Box," p. 13). Use 80–220-grit sandpaper to sand both sides of the disk smooth (see "Sanding," p. 13).

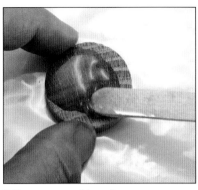

2 Because wood is quite porous, a quick coat of resin will prevent colored resin from bleeding into areas where it shouldn't. Apply a thin coat of resin to one side of the disk. Cover and allow the resin to cure.

3 Flip the disk over, apply resin, and cure.

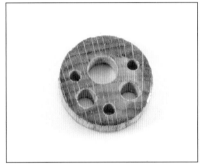

4 Use several sizes of drill bits and drill holes at least ⅛ in. (3mm) from the edge of the disk (see "Drilling," p. 13).

5 Use your finger to burnish a piece of packaging tape to the back of the disk to create a tight seal.

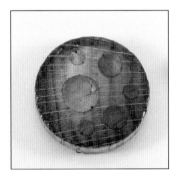

6 Use a toothpick to drop dyed resin into the drilled holes of the disk. Lightly tap the disk on the table to help bubbles rise to the surface, and remove. Cover and allow the resin to cure.

7 Remove the tape, find the center of the disk, and mark with a permanent marker (see "Finding the Center of a Circle," p. 14).

8 Using the centerpoint as a guide, draw a line across the disk. Use the saw and miter box to cut the disk in half.

9 Use 80–400-grit sandpaper to smooth and flatten both cut surfaces of the disk.

If you'd like to seal the cut edge of wood with a coat of resin, now would be the best time to do so.

10 Place a large inner diameter jump ring over the edge of the half circle. Along the edge, mark the entry and exit points needed to use for that ring. Starting with a smaller drill bit than you need for the final hole, drill a hole in the rounded edge of the disk toward the cut edge of the disk (see "Drilling," p. 13). You can either drill halfway and then drill from the flat edge, joining both holes, or continue drilling from the domed edge and adjust the angle (if needed) with each drill bit to align with the marked exit point. Once the hole is drilled, step up a bit size and re-drill, slowly enlarging the hole. Repeat until the hole is large enough for the jump ring.

11 Thread the jump ring through the component, add the earring wire, and close the ring (see "Jewelry Basics, p. 14).
12 Repeat steps 10 and 11 to drill and string the second component to make another earring the mirror image of the first.

PROJECT 19

Base Block Bracelet

After purchasing my first house, one of my first home improvement projects was replacing all the woodwork. It went from ugly laminate to gorgeously finished colonial-style trim. The rosettes, plinth blocks, and crown molding really dressed up the place, and by using all those pre-cut blocks, we didn't need to worry about mitering the corners together—which, in turn sped up the whole process. So, while you can purchase wood and then cut it into a square dowel, starting with a pre-fabricated base block is a quicker and easier alternative.

Resin Component Supplies
- Oak or hardwood inside base block
- Pencil and ruler
- Saw/miter box
- Sandpaper
- Resin
- Resin dye
- Packaging tape
- Drill/drill bits
- Sponge brush or craft stick

Jewelry Supplies
- **14** large jump rings
- **20** small jump rings
- Clasp
- **2** pairs chainnose pliers

1 Select an inside base block in oak. Sand the end of the base block smooth and level working through 80–220-grit sandpaper (see "Sanding," p. 13).

2 Use a pencil and a ruler to mark ¼ in. (6mm) from the bottom of the block.

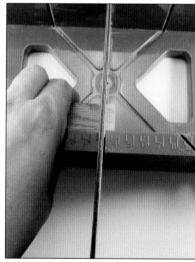

3 Use your saw and miter box (see "Using a Miter Box," p. 13) to cut through the block at the ¼-in. (6mm) mark.

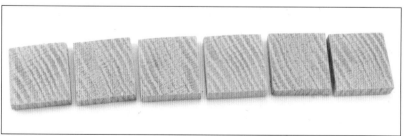

4 Sand the fresh cut side of the square, and the base block smooth and level, working through 80–220-grit sandpaper. Set the cut square aside.
5 Repeat steps 2–4 until you have 6–8 sanded squares of wood.

It doesn't take much effort to create a spare square, and I find it helpful to have a backup or two.

6 Because of the porous nature of wood, keep colored resin from seeping into spaces it shouldn't by applying a light coat of resin on all sides to prevent bleed-through. Use a sponge brush or craft stick to apply a coat of resin to the four edges of the square. Then set the square down on a plastic surface, and apply a coat of resin to the front of the square. Cover and allow to cure.

7 Once cured, flip the pieces over and apply a coat of resin to the back of the squares. Cover and allow to cure.

Although you can coat all sides and set the square on plastic to dry, I've found that allowing the fronts and backs of the squares to cure separately means I have less sanding clean up in the long run.

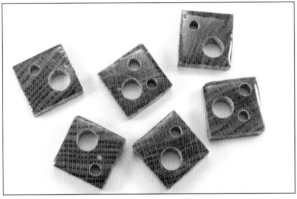

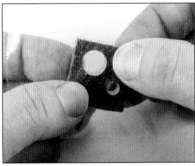

8 Using a variety of drill bit sizes, drill two or three holes into each of the squares (see "Drilling" p. 13). Keep at least 1/8 in. (3mm) from the edge of the square, and don't let the holes get too close together.

9 Use your fingers to burnish a piece of packaging tape to the back side of each square. The tape creates a temporary back to your wooden bezel.

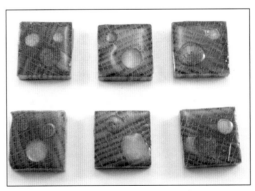

10 Use a toothpick, colored resin, and a steady hand to fill up roughly half of the drilled bezels. Mix a second color of resin and fill up all the remaining bezels. Lightly tap the squares on the table to help any trapped air bubbles rise to the surface, and remove them. Cover and allow the resin to cure.

It's OK if some of the resin overflows its bezel. Try to avoid mixing the colors, but use a baby wipe to clean up what you can. The rest can be sanded off later.

11 Remove the tape from the squares. Use a variety of drill bits to make two or three various sizes of holes in each square. Drill into the cured resin to create overlapping circles of color.

12 Burnish fresh packaging tape to the bottoms of the squares to create a tight seal, and pour two more colors of resin into the drilled bezels. Cover and allow to cure.

13 Remove the packaging tape and check that the resin level is flush with the wood. If the tape wasn't completely sealed, or there was a large air bubble that escaped, you will see a concave bezel like this green resin. You can either try to color-match and fill in that little trough, or you can add just a bit of clear resin to bring the level flush with the wooden face. Cover and allow to cure.

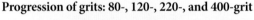

Progression of grits: 80-, 120-, 220-, and 400-grit

14 Use 80–400-grit sandpaper to sand the squares and make the resin and the wood one flush surface (see "Sanding," p. 13). You may expose raw wood in some spots, depending on how level your resin is and how much you sand. Rinse and scrub the squares thoroughly with an old toothbrush and running water. Pat dry with a soft cloth.

15 Use a sponge brush to apply a thin coat of resin to seal any exposed wood. Cover and allow to cure.

16 The finish is a matter of personal preference. You can stop here and leave the squares with a shiny finish, sand with 1500-grit to create more of an eggshell finish, or use a rougher grit if you prefer a frosted look. The sample was given a once-over with 1500-grit.

17 Staying at least ⅛ in. (3mm) from the edge, drill holes for jump rings (see "Drilling," p. 13). I varied the number of holes, but in hindsight, the center squre should have been drilled twice to coordinate better with the end squares (another reason it's a good idea to make a spare square). Connect the jump rings with three-jump ring rosettes or plain jump rings (see "Weaving Rosettes," p. 33, to create rosettes, and "Jewelry Basics," p. 14).

 If you choose a sanded finish, use a light touch. If you expose raw wood, apply another coat of resin and re-sand.

TIP Any extra squares can be used for earrings or a pendant.

PROJECT 20

Jellyfish Pendant

While working at *Art Jewelry* magazine, I was sent an image of an amethyst that held a jellyfish. Sure, I had seen my fair share of bugs encased in amber, but it was amazing to see a tiny jellyfish suspended in that purple stone. It was like a tiny, magical aquarium and that jellyfish would start moving any second.

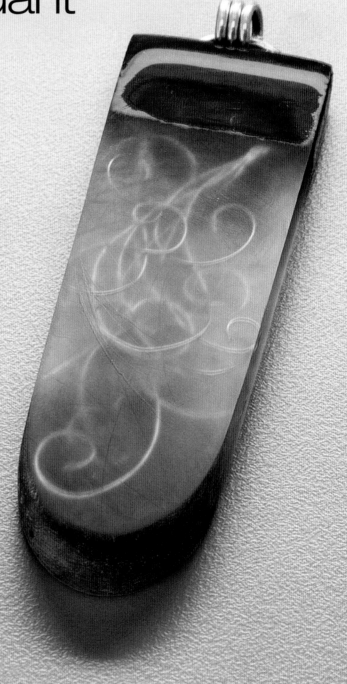

WHAT YOU'LL NEED

Resin Component Supplies
- Wood: African Padauk, or other type of hardwood
- Saw
- Sandpaper, 80–2000-grit
- Permanent marker and ruler
- Drill/drill bits
- Coated picture wire
- Heavy-duty wire cutters
- Wire stripper or utility knife
- Roundnose pliers or mandrel
- White glue, or other clear-drying glue
- Toothpicks
- Molding compound
- Packaging tape
- Scrap lath or wood
- Clamp
- Resin
- Resin dye
- Scissors or craft knife

Jewelry Supplies
- **3** jump rings
- **2** pairs chainnose pliers

1 Cut and sand (80–220-grit) a small piece of African Padauk or other hardwood into a rectangle (roughly ⁷⁄₈x½x¼ in./22x13x6mm).

2 Use a ruler and a permanent marker to mark drill two holes on the top and bottom of the rectangle where desired.

3 Use a small drill bit and drill through the wood (see "Drilling," p. 13). If you don't think you can drill a straight hole through the wood, drill part way into the top holes, then flip over and drill part way from the bottom. Keep flipping and drilling a little further until the two sides meet up.

TIP Only one of these drilled surfaces will ever be seen. If the hole is not perfectly parallel, it can easily be camouflaged under the resin.

4 Use a heavy-duty wire cutters (you don't want to potentially damage your jewelry wire cutters) to cut a 12–18-in. (30–46cm) piece of coated picture wire.

5 Thread the wire through the drilled rectangle of wood. Pull the wire snugly, but make sure you can still fit jump rings or other connectors to attach the finished pendant to a necklace.

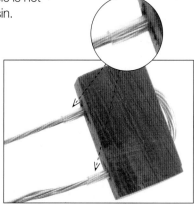

6 Using either a wire stripper or a utility knife, remove the plastic coating from the wire, leaving less than ¼ in. (6mm) of coating below the wood.

USING A WIRE STRIPPER

Find the hole in the jaws of the wire stripper that is just slightly smaller than the diameter of the wire. Place the last ½–1 in. (1.3–2.5cm) end of the wire in that depression and gently squeeze the jaw shut, cutting into the plastic **[A]**. Open the jaw, rotate the wire 90 degrees and close again, cutting the plastic coating again. Holding the jaws closed, pull the wire stripper away from the wire, thereby pulling off the cut section of coating **[B]**. Repeat until the desired length of coating is removed.

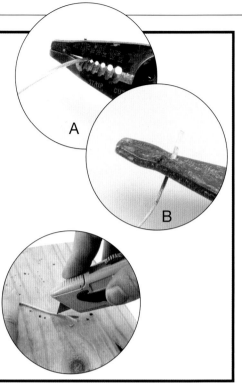

 If you are having problems pulling off the coating, check to see if you are cutting all the way through the coating. Or try cutting off smaller sections.

USING A UTILITY KNIFE

Place the wire on a piece of scrap wood and press it firmly in place with your non-dominant hand. Use a utility knife in your dominant hand to cut a line through the plastic coating.

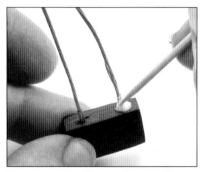

7 Use a toothpick to apply a small amount of clear-drying glue between the coated picture wire and the wood. When the glue dries, it acts like a plug and won't allow any resin to seep through the holes. Clean up any excess glue, and set aside until the glue dries.

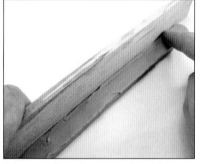

8 Create a long flat strip of molding compound. The length will be determined by how long you want to make the pendant. The strip I'm using is about 8 in. (20cm) long (see "Using Two-Part Silicone Molding Compound, p. 10).

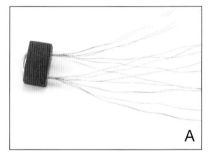

9 Once the glue is dry, untwist the picture wire **[A]**. Use a combination of your fingers, roundnose pliers, or mandrel pliers, and wire cutters to trim, curl, and wave the individual wires into a form no denser than the width and depth of the wooden rectangle, and between 1–2 in. (2.5–5cm) long **[B]**.

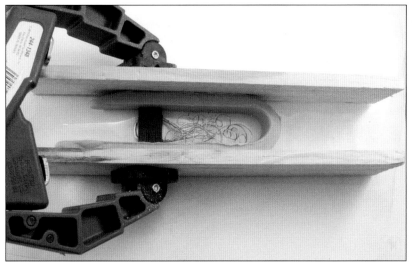

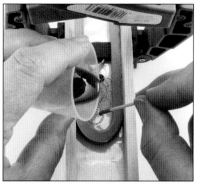

10 Secure the wooden rectangle on a piece of packaging tape. Wrap the strip of cured molding compound into a U-shape around the curled wires of the component. Press the flat edge of the molding compound into the packaging tape. Place pieces of scrap wood on either side of the U-shape to keep the sides of the pendant level. Place the clamp on either side of the wooden rectangle.

11 Pour colored resin into the bottom of the pendant and clear resin towards the wooden rectangle along the top (see "Coloring Resin," p. 11). You can allow them to naturally mix, or try to swirl them together by using toothpicks. Keep in mind you want to be able to see the wire swirls, so add in the colored resin gradually.

12 Cover and allow the resin to dry (see "Dry Time vs. Cure Time," p. 12).

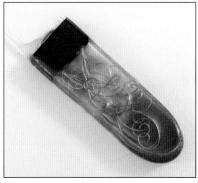

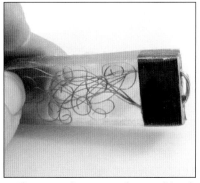

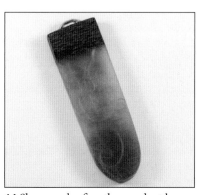

13 Remove the form. Use a scissors to trim off any overflow. Use a fine craft knife to cut away any resin between the wood and the bail wire, taking care not to cut away the plastic coating on the wire. If the resin is concave or not level with the wooden rectangle, you can add clear resin until the piece is level. Cover and allow to cure.

14 Shape and refine the pendant by sanding with 80-grit sandpaper (see "Sanding," p. 13).

15 To create the "frosted glass" effect, sand the entire piece up to 400-grit.

16 Continue sanding the front of the piece to 2000-grit for a clear, yet "soft-focus" effect. If you prefer a crystal-clear front, you can add another layer of resin. And to bring out the color of the wood you can apply a thin coat of resin; just be sure not to get any on the "frosted" resin, or it will turn crystal clear and need to be resanded.

17 Attach three jump rings to the pendant (see "Jewelry Basics," p. 14).

BONUS PROJECT

Fingerprint Pendants

This is a great project that can easily be customized into mother jewelry or two prints on a necklace to represent a couple (cute gift idea for newlyweds). You can also swap print pendants with your best friend.

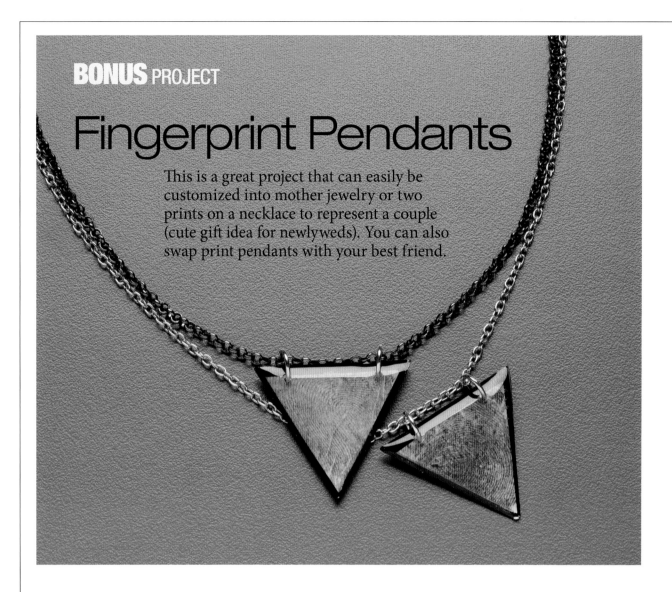

WHAT YOU'LL NEED

Resin Component Supplies
- Heavy stock paper
- Ink pad
- Scissors and/or paper punch
- Glue stick
- Resin
- Craft stick
- Ruler and pencil (optional)
- Drill/drill bits

Jewelry Supplies
- **2** jump rings
- Chain with clasp or cord
- **2** pairs chainnose pliers

1 Get a clean fingerprint on paper. This step might be easier said than done (as I discovered when trying to get prints from my four-year-old; eventually, I gave up and recruited my husband instead). One color print is fine, but I wanted the fingerprints to be two-tone, so I started with the lighter ink (orange) and generously spread it onto the thumb, making sure to get into all the grooves of the print. Then I lightly dabbed the darker color (red) over the thumb to highlight the raised ridges.

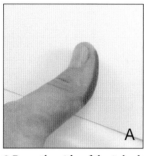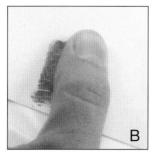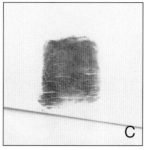

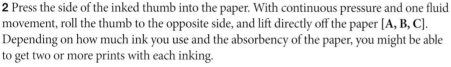

2 Press the side of the inked thumb into the paper. With continuous pressure and one fluid movement, roll the thumb to the opposite side, and lift directly off the paper [**A, B, C**]. Depending on how much ink you use and the absorbency of the paper, you might be able to get two or more prints with each inking.

TIP

Work close to the edge of your work surface and practice rolling the thumb/ finger to find the best placement for the paper.

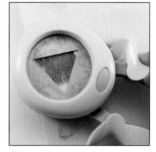

3 Since white paper will go slightly transparent when resin is applied (like water on white clothing), apply a light coat of white acrylic paint to the backside of the paper under the fingerprint. Let the paint dry.

4 Use scissors or a paper punch to cut out the fingerprint.

5 Since I want to remove all the blank white paper from the print and I only have one size triangle punch, I used a ruler and pencil to crop out as much white space as possible and trimmed with scissors.

6 Use the same punch or a pair of scissors to cut a triangle out of black cardstock. Apply a liberal amount of glue from a glue stick to adhere the layers together. Compress and burnish the layers together to drive out any trapped air bubbles. Allow to dry.

TIP

If needed, use a toothpick to push the resin to coat the tips of the triangle.

7 Apply a layer of resin to the back of the triangle. Cover and allow to cure.

8 Flip the triangle over and apply a coat of resin to the front of the triangle. Cover and allow to cure. If you discover any air bubbles in your cured piece, see steps 17 and 18 from "Pipe Bail Pendant," p. 37, to remove them.

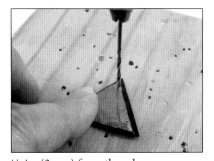

9 Since I layered my resin on fairly thick, two coats is enough to make a sturdy pendant. However, check the tips of the triangle (both sides) and the coverage, then determine if an additional coat, or two, should be applied to your piece. Staying at least

$1/8$ in. (3mm) from the edges, use a permanent marker and a ruler to mark placement for drill holes.

10 Use a small drill bit to drill holes in the pendant (see "Drilling," p. 13).

11 Add jump rings and secure the pendant to a chain (see "Jewelry Basics," p. 14).

DOG PRINTS

Did you know that dog nose prints are as unique as human fingerprints? While I won't recommend trying to ink any dog noses, you can make a quick "nose stamp" with the help of a little molding compound.

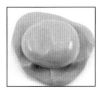

1 Mix the molding compound per manufacturer's instructions (see "Using Two-Part Silicone Molding Compound," p. 10). Use a quick-set compound; you don't want to endanger the dog by restricting its airway while the compound sets. Form into a disk shape and press onto the dog's nose, for a quick count to five. Remove the molding compound and place on a flat surface to cure.

2 Mix a second batch of molding compound and press it onto the negative nose mold. Set aside and allow it to set up.

3 Gently peel the layers apart.

TIP Do NOT hold the dog's mouth shut while doing this or they will panic, potentially endangering you and the dog.

4 You now have a replica of your dog's nose print pattern and you can ink and stamp to your heart's delight. Use baby wipes, or rubbing alcohol on a paper towel to remove any excess ink from your new stamp.

BONUS PROJECT

Beveled Paper Pendant

This simple pendant design is easy to customize with your school or team colors. Its sleek design can stand on its own, or use it as the canvas for a collage or favorite image. See "Retro Targets Pendant," p. 46, to learn how to make a multi-colored brick of paper, which is the starting point for this project.

WHAT YOU'LL NEED

Resin Component Supplies
- Multi-colored paper brick
- Resin
- Craft stick and sponge brush
- Saw/miter box
- Permanent marker
- Ruler
- Sandpaper
- Drill/drill bits
- Third hand and toothpick (optional)

Jewelry Supplies
- **2** jump rings
- **2** pairs chainnose pliers
- Finished neck chain

1 Using your saw and miter box cut a straight edge along one side of the paper brick (see "Using a Miter Box," p. 13). Use 80-grit sandpaper to smooth and refine the cut edge.

2 Pressing your straight cut edge against the miter box edge, trim a second side of the brick, creating a 90-degree angle. Use 80-grit sandpaper to smooth and refine the cut edge.

3 Determine how wide you want the pendant to be and mark with a ruler and permanent marker. Use the saw and miter box to cut the brick. Sand with 80-grit sandpaper to smooth and refine the cut edge.

TIP Before cutting, determine the front of the component and align it in the miter box accordingly (see "Using a Miter Box," p. 13).

4 Determine how long the pendant should be and mark with a ruler and permanent marker. Use the saw and miter box to cut a 45-degree angle off the bottom of the component. Use 80-grit sandpaper to smooth and refine the beveled edge.

5 Depending on the final finish desired, you may want to use 400-grit (or higher) sandpaper to lightly sand the front and back of the component.

TIP If you press too hard or are too abrasive with the sandpaper, you will begin to sand through the layers of paper, which could be great if you want a more "distressed" look.

6 Use a permanent marker and a ruler to mark where the jump rings will be placed on the pendant.

7 Use a drill and drill bits to drill through the component (see "Drilling," p. 13).

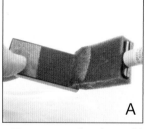

A

B

8 Use a sponge brush to add a light coat of resin to all sides of the pendant [**A**], and fully suspend the pendant using a third hand and a toothpick or some other suspension method to cure [**B**].

9 For more of an eggshell finish and to see the layers on the edges better, use 1500-grit sandpaper to wet-sand the edges of the pendant.

10 For a high-gloss finish on the front of the pendant, add a light coat of resin and allow to cure. Be sure to not get any resin in the drilled holes, and clean up any overflow along the edges.

TIP Make sure you don't get any resin on the toothpick, or it may bond to the pendant.

If you have no way to suspend the pendant, you might want to only coat a few sides, place the uncoated side down, allow to dry, then coat the rest of the pendant. If you coat the entire pendant and place it on plastic, you may have to trim off some overflow and will get some texture from the plastic.

11 Add jump rings to suspend the pendant from a cord or chain (see "Jewelry Basics," p. 14).

From the Author

The biggest and most important thank you is for my husband, Brit. Whether it was running out to pick up last-minute supplies, getting up in the middle of the night to help me shoot "just a couple more" images, or distracting the kids with extended out-of-the-house adventures, you've helped keep me focused on finishing my second book. I don't know where I'd be without you. I love you.

Thank you to my parents, Don and Nadine Drake, for teaching me the value of hard work, dedication, and the joy of learning and creativity. But most importantly, the value and need for compassion in this crazy world. Because of this, a portion from all royalties received from this book will be donated to help animals in need. A special thank you to my grandparents, Gilbert and Rita, for letting me raid their old photos; DJ, Scottie, Jeff, and Pam, just because sometimes nagging really does get things done (right Pam?); and to my nieces Camryn, Kaden, Kendra, and Hadley for just being themselves.

Deb Simon, who first introduced me to this crazy-fun world of resin; Dianne Wheeler and my Editor, Erica Swanson for being willing to work with me again and accommodating my crazy schedule; and William Zuback, Lisa Bergman, and the rest of the Art staff, who once again impress and flatter me by making my words and work look absolutely fabulous! Thanks to my past work family, for believing in me enough to give me a chance, whether it was encouraging me directly or bending the ear of someone else who helped get me to the next step, especially Jane Bremmer, Dawn Becker, Lori Schneider, Cathy Jakicic, Hazel Wheaton, Linda Kast, Julia Gerlach, Jill Erickson, Annie Pennington, Allison Salkeld, and Annie Guldberg.

To so many people who where there for me when I needed you most, your help, encouragement and sometimes just plain fun distractions helped me maintain/regain sanity, perspective, and creativity through some "interesting" times; Karen Kostan, Wendy Bronstad, Bill and Cindy Barder, Eliana Knapp, Anne Bates, Eric McGaughy, and all my fellow fire troupe members with Brewcity Fire Brigade. And to Mr. Bag-O-Donuts, wherever you are.

And last, but not least, thank you to everyone who bought my first book, *Play With Chain Mail,* and/or took one of my classes. Meeting so many kindred jewelry makers, artists, and writers has been one of my favorite parts of this journey. Thank you!

About the Author

Theresa was raised in a small Wisconsin town. Influenced by her mother's freeform approach to exploring new hobbies and her father's logical "measure-twice-cut-once" mechanical inclinations, it's no wonder Theresa has followed her creative endeavors—no matter where they might lead her. She has an eclectic combination of backgrounds ranging from Apiarist Assistant, to Graphic Designer, to Animal Control Officer, to Firefighter/EMT, to Assistant Editor at *Art Jewelry* magazine, to Author (Theresa's first book, *Play With Chain Mail*, was released in 2016), to Stay-At-Home Mom (by far the most rigorous job to date!).

With an audio book blasting away, she can be found working on various jewelry, chain mail, photography, or [insert-latest-hobby-experiment-here] projects. When she does get out of the studio, she can be found either playing with her children, working on yet another home improvement project, or performing with her fire troupe, the Brewcity Fire Brigade. She lives in Milwaukee with her husband, their two children, and a small menagerie of rescued animals.

Visit Theresa's website at TDAbelew.com, find her on Facebook, and follow her (@TDAbelew) on Instagram & Twitter.

Photo credits
Process Photos: Theresa D. Abelew and Briton M. Abelew

Learn a New Jewelry Technique!

The *Absolute Beginners Guide* series is the perfect way to immerse yourself in all types of jewelry making. Learn everything you need to know about these fun and popular jewelry techniques. You'll want to get started right away!

The Absolute Beginners Guide: Making Chain Mail Jewelry • Item #64803

The Absolute Beginners Guide: Working with Polymer Clay • Item #64537

The Absolute Beginners Guide: Stringing Beaded Jewelry • Item #62991

Buy now from your favorite craft or bead shop!
Shop at JewelryandBeadingStore.com

KALMBACH BOOKS